Big Book of 3-Minute Bible Story Activities

This book is a compilation of previously published materials.

Cover Illustration by Judy Hierstein
Cover Production by Nehmen-Kodner

A Division of Frank Schaffer Publications, Inc.
23740 Hawthorne Blvd., Torrance, CA 90505

Table of Contents

Introduction

This book is a great way for children to learn about a wonderful variety of Bible stories in short periods of time.

The Old and New Testament stories included feature Creation, Adam and Eve, Abraham, Isaac, Jacob, Joseph's Coat, Moses and the Trip to the Promised Land, David and Goliath, Samson, Jesus' Birth, John the Baptist, Jesus in the Temple, Jesus Calming the Storm, Jesus' Death on the Cross, the Resurrection, and so much more! If time allows, read the children not only the story versions in this book, but the Bible passages as well.

Following each story are meaningful and stimulating activities, such as simple crafts, songs, fingerplays, poems, games, choral readings, recipes, creative writing ideas, and many others. (Also included are bulletin board ideas, Bible verses for memorization, and any necessary patterns, among other things.) Each activity and idea has been designed to reinforce details of the story it is based on and to give children opportunities to display Christian values.

Whether you choose to use the stories and activities in this book for Sunday school use, to supplement other areas of study, for home use, or for another reason, you are sure to enjoy watching children listen, sing, and play as they learn about God's love for us.

God Made It All

Genesis 1:1–2:7

Long ago, there was no world. There was only darkness and God. Then God decided to make a very special place. On the first day of His labors, He divided the darkness, making light which He called "day" and dark which He called "night."

Next, God commanded that there be a sky above which was filled with clean, fresh air. This was the second day. On the third day, God formed the waters below the sky into great seas. Then He made dry ground appear and He called it "land."

On the fourth day, God did a wondrous thing. He made the land bring forth all kinds of vegetation: seed-bearing trees, fruits, bushes, flowers, green grass. This new world was becoming very beautiful! Next, He looked up into the sky and He "decorated" it. In the night sky, He put stars and a moon. In the day sky, He placed a bright sun.

As the fifth day dawned, God set about putting living things on His new world. He made fish for the seas. He made birds to fly in the sky.

On the sixth day, God made the animals that walk upon the land and live in the forests and jungles He had created. Finally, God decided His new world needed one more thing—people. God in His wisdom and love made man and woman. He gave them the new world and all that was in it. It was theirs to care for.

On the seventh day, God looked at all He had created and declared it was good. God blessed this day and called it holy. Then God rested.

Creation Mobile

This mobile is a great way to help children remember the story of creation.

Materials:

copies of the patterns below, paper, glue or tape, coat hangers, scissors, yarn, magazines

Directions:

Make a copy of the patterns below for each child. Have them cut out the patterns. Then have the children cut out pictures from magazines that depict the beautiful world God made. They can glue their pictures and the patterns on large sheets of paper. Have the children cut out the pictures. They can glue or tape yarn to the back of each picture and attach the pictures to a coat hanger.

sun

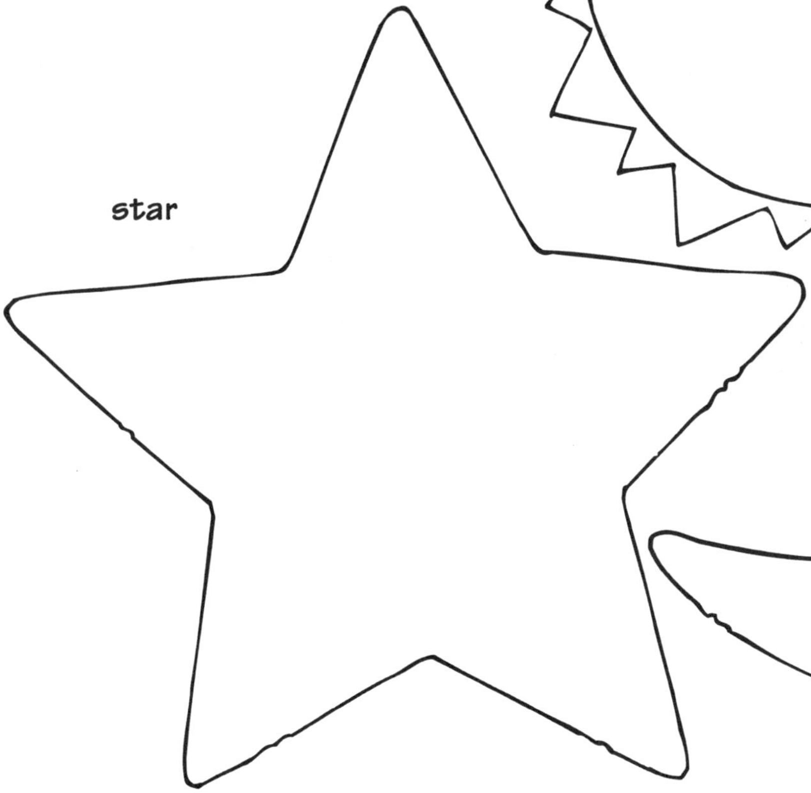

star

moon

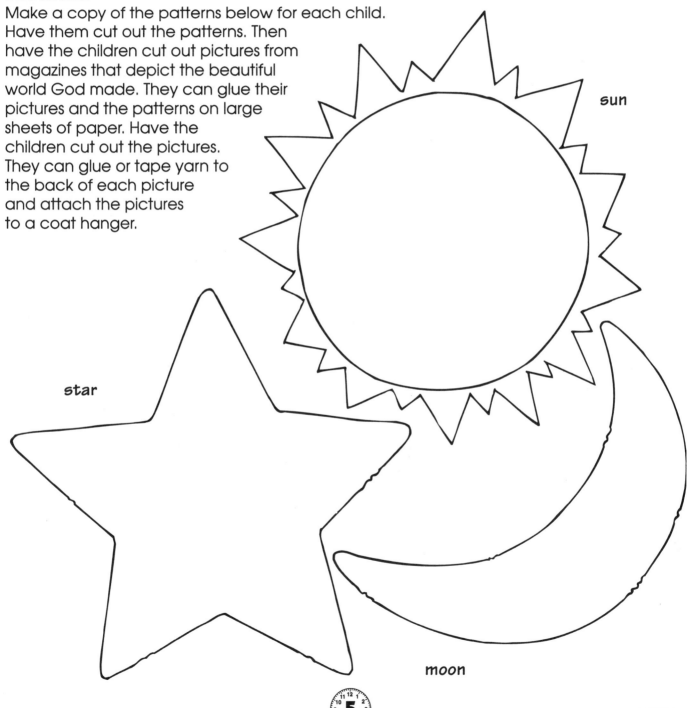

Shadow Box

Shadow boxes are a lot of fun for the children to make and help reinforce the story of creation.

Materials:

patterns (pages 7–8)
blue construction paper
greenery, soil, and pebbles (optional)
shoeboxes
tape or glue
scissors
string
markers or crayons

Directions:

Let the children use shoeboxes to create the world. Tell them to line their boxes with blue construction paper. Then give each child a copy of the patterns on pages 7–8. The children can then color and cut out the patterns. Next, they place the cutouts in their shoeboxes in the order in which God created them. They can hang the sun, moon, and clouds with stars and birds from the top of the shoebox using string and tape. Real greenery, soil, and pebbles may be added for a special look. Have the children place the man and woman in the front.

Patterns

Fold.

Tab

Fold.

Fold.

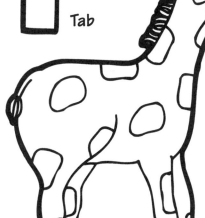

Patterns

Fold.

Fold.

Fold.

The Sneaky Snake

Genesis 3

God prepared a beautiful garden for the man and woman He had created. He told them they could eat any fruit except that which grew on the tree in the center of the garden. God warned them that the fruit of that tree would bring death.

One day, a sneaky snake slithered into the garden. It silently slunk up into a swaying tree and settled down. The man and woman came walking by, and the sneaky snake smiled and asked, "Did God really tell you that you could not eat any of the fruit?"

The woman replied, "We cannot eat from the tree in the middle of the garden. It is deadly!"

The sneaky snake snickered and said, "He's lying to you. He simply doesn't want you to be as smart as He is."

The woman thought for a moment, then picked a fruit from the tree and took a big bite. The sneaky snake smiled. The woman told the man to take a bite. He did! The sneaky snake was filled with supreme satisfaction.

Later, God asked the man and woman what they had done. The man blamed the woman, and the woman blamed the sneaky snake. God was angry. He told the sneaky snake that he would be forever hated. Then God sent the man and woman out of the beautiful garden and said they could never return.

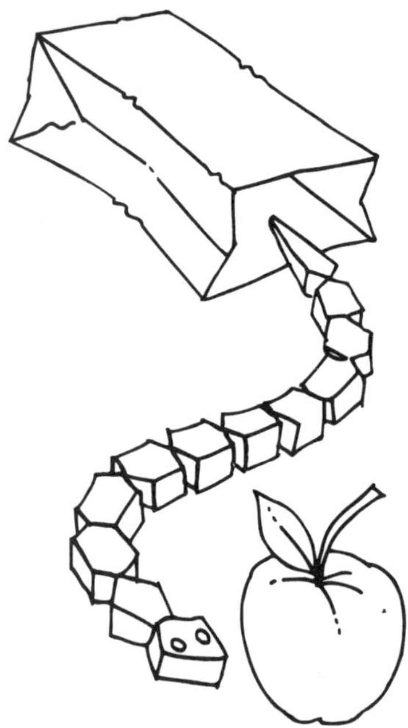

Have the children memorize the Bible verse below. Discuss times when they have been deceived. How did they feel? How do they think God felt?

The woman said, "The serpent deceived me, and I ate." (Genesis 3:13b)

What a Sneak!

Materials:
rubber snake, apple, small paper bag

Directions:
With the snake and apple in a paper bag, read or tell in your own words the story on page 9. Emphasize the *S* words so that they sound like the hissing of a snake. When the snake appears in the story, pull out the rubber snake from the bag. When the woman picks the fruit, remove the apple and take a bite. Repeat for the man.

Temptation

Print the word "temptation" in large letters on the board or a piece of paper. Ask the children what this word means. Continue by asking them to share times when they have been tempted to do something they knew was wrong.

Egg Carton Snake

Materials:
snake patterns to the right
Styrofoam™ egg cartons
pipe cleaners
scissors
crayons
glue

Directions:
Cut out six individual egg cups for each child. Help the children connect the cups with short pieces of pipe cleaner. Reproduce the snake patterns for each child. Tell the children to color them and then glue the head and tongue to the first cup and the tail to the last, gluing on the tabs.

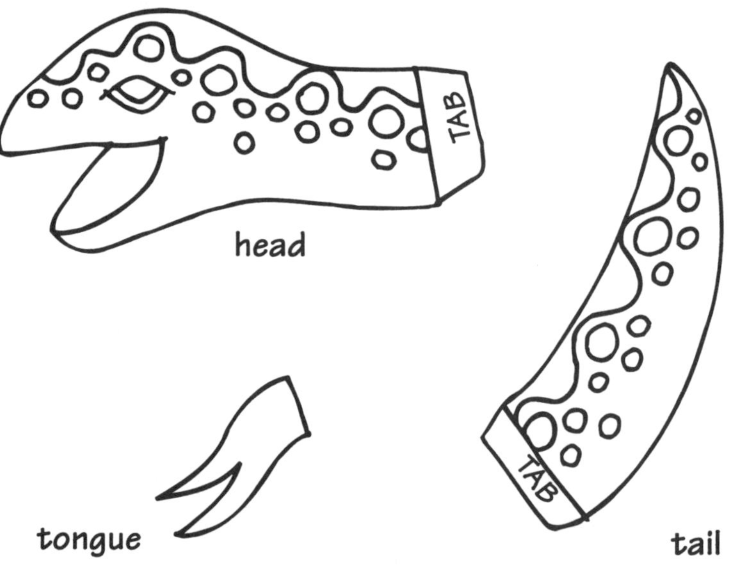

Stick Puppets

These are fun for children to use to act out the events in the Garden of Eden.

Materials:

- patterns from this page
- markers or crayons
- craft sticks
- glue
- scissors

Directions:

Have the children color and cut out the figures on this page and glue them to craft sticks. They can use the puppets to show what happened in the Garden of Eden.

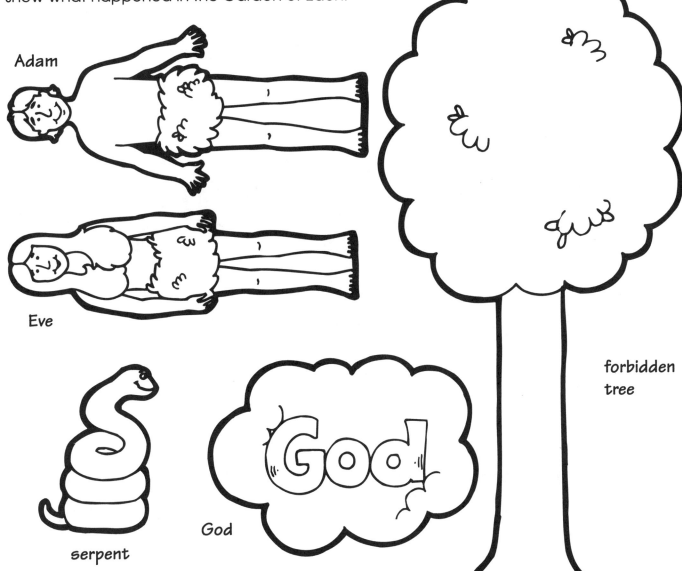

Adam

Eve

forbidden tree

serpent

God

The Big Flood

Genesis 6:11–9:17

Back in the days of Noah, there was much wickedness and violence on the earth. The people were doing things that were against God's will. God decided to get rid of the people because of their violence against Him.

Noah was the only person on earth who was honoring God, and God wanted to save him. God told Noah that He was going to destroy the earth with a flood. He told Noah to make an ark out of cypress wood. It was to be 450' long and 75' wide. That would make the ark longer than a football field but not quite as wide.

The Big Flood continued

God told Noah to cover the ark with pitch, build on a roof, make three decks (lower, middle, and top), and put a door in one side. He also told Noah to bring his wife, his sons and their wives, and a male and female of every animal aboard the ark. This was to include birds and the things that crawl on the earth. Noah was also told to bring a lot of food for the animals and the people.

Noah did exactly as God had told him. Then the Lord shut him, his family, and the animals into the ark.

Noah was 600 years old when the rain began. On the day he finished loading the ark, God shut him in and rain gushed down from the heavens. It rained for 40 days and 40 nights.

The whole face of the earth was flooded. Even the highest mountains were covered. Everything that lived on the earth died. Even birds, which usually fly above water, did not survive that flood. The flood lasted 150 days.

Noah and his family took care of the animals for the whole trip. He finally sent a raven out of the ark to check on things. The raven flew around until the water had dried up and it could land.

After a while, Noah sent out a dove. The dove came back. He waited seven more days, then sent the dove out again. Finally, the dove came back. In its beak was a freshly picked olive leaf! This meant that the water had gone down enough for some treetops to be visible. Noah and his family were very happy.

Noah waited another seven days, then sent the dove out again. This time, it didn't return. God had sent a wind, and the waters were dried from off the earth. He told Noah, *"Come out of the ark, you and your wife, and your sons and their wives. Bring out every kind of living creature that is with you—the birds, the animals, and all the creatures that move along the ground—so that they can multiply on the earth . . ."* (Genesis 9:16–17)

Noah did as he was told. He built an altar to the Lord and burnt offerings on it.

God told Noah that He would never again flood the entire earth. As a sign of that promise, He put a rainbow in the sky for Noah and for the rest of us, too. The next time we see a rainbow, let's think of God's promise and His mercy to Noah and to us. We wouldn't be here today if long, long ago, God hadn't saved a few people from that flood.

Have the children memorize the Bible verses below. They can also write them on sheets of paper or on mural paper and illustrate them.

Noah did everything just as God commanded him. (Genesis 6:22)

"I have set my rainbow in the clouds." (Genesis 9:13a)

A Colorful World

Gather these seven colors of crayons: red, orange, yellow, green, blue, indigo, violet. Hold up each crayon. Ask each child to name something in God's world that is each color. Ask them to look around the room and find things that are these seven colors. Explain that the beautiful rainbow God created contains all of these colors.

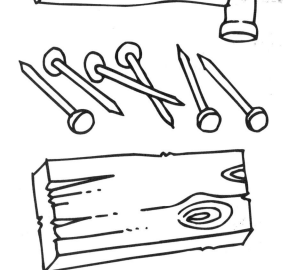

God's Tools

This activity helps children learn about special people who helped God.

Materials: large sheets of paper, various tools (from a child's tool set would be best)

Have each child choose a tool, place it on paper, and trace around it. When the papers are covered with tool outlines, have children print names of people in the Bible who were led by God to do difficult things. Noah should be their first choice. Others might include Jesus, David, Gideon, Elijah, Moses, etc.

God's Rainbow

These rainbows make nice reminders of God's promise to never flood earth again.

Materials: the rainbow and cloud patterns on page 15; yarn, glitter, small buttons, sequins, lace, ribbon, etc., in the seven colors of a rainbow

Reproduce the rainbow and cloud patterns for each child. Let the children use the materials to make rainbows, using the seven colors mentioned in the story. Have them fill in each of the rainbow arcs in order, beginning with red and ending with violet. Show them how to cut out the two clouds and glue one at each end of the completed rainbow.

Patterns

rainbow

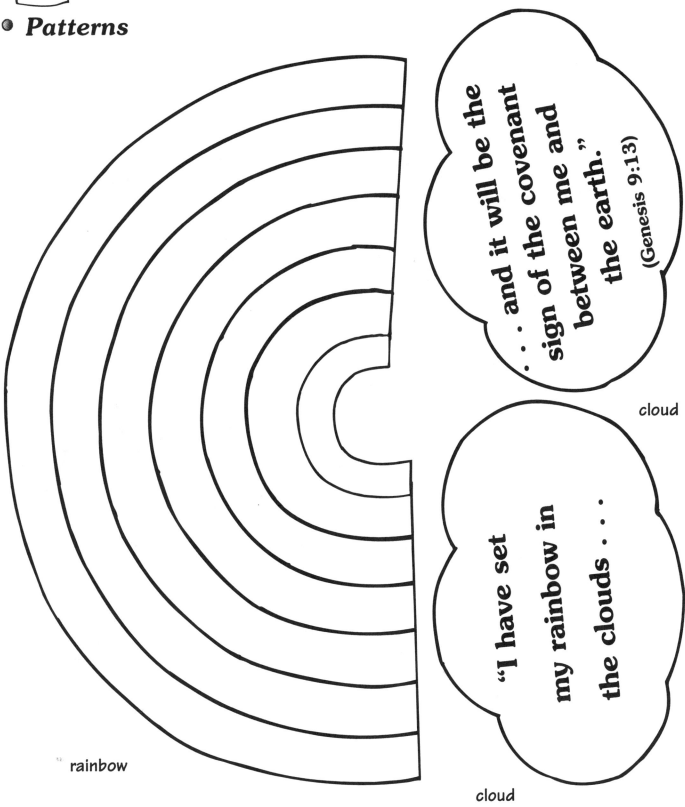

". . . and it will be the
sign of the covenant
between me and
the earth."
(Genesis 9:13)

cloud

"I have set
my rainbow in
the clouds . . ."

cloud

Animal Matching Game

This game is great fun for children to play and improves memory skills and animal recognition.

Materials: 2 copies of this page and page 17, posterboard, glue, scissors

Glue the copies of pages 16 and 17 on posterboard and cut out the cards. The game is played like "Go Fish." Shuffle the cards. Pass out five cards to each player. The players try to make pairs. A player asks the person on his or her right, "Do you have an elephant (or any card that will allow him or her to make a pair)?" If the person has an elephant, he or she gives it to the player, and the player gets another turn. If the person does not have an elephant, he or she says, "Go ask Noah." The player then draws a card from the pile. If the card is an elephant, the player gets another turn. If the card is not an elephant, the person on the right takes his or her turn. Pairs should be put facedown on the table. The player with the most pairs at the end of the game wins.

lion	monkey	bear
giraffe	zebra	lamb

Animal Matching Game continued

bird	tiger	butterfly
hippopotamus	kangaroo	elephant
rhinoceros	camel	rabbit

Come See

Have the children sing these words to the tune of "Go Tell Aunt Rhodie" using the appropriate motions.

Come see the rainbow.	*(Beckon with both hands.)*
Come see the rainbow.	*(Beckon with both hands.)*
Come see the rainbow.	*(Beckon with both hands.)*
God put up in the sky.	*(Arch both arms over head.)*
It's above the houses.	*(Point up with right hand.)*
It's above the treetops.	*(Point up with left hand.)*
It's above the mountains.	*(Point up with right hand again.)*
It's way up in the sky.	*(Arch both arms over head.)*
The rainbow is God's promise.	*(Clasp hands in pray position.)*
The rainbow is God's promise.	*(Clasp hands in pray position.)*
The rainbow is God's promise.	*(Clasp hands in pray position.)*
He soon will make things dry.	*(Nod head.)*
Come see the rainbow.	*(Beckon with both hands.)*
Come see the rainbow.	*(Beckon with both hands.)*
Come see the rainbow.	*(Beckon with both hands.)*
God put up in the sky.	*(Arch both arms over head.)*

A Pretty Picture

Make copies of the picture below. Have the children color the picture. They should also color the back of the bottom portion blue. Next, help them cut out the picture on the bold lines. Have the children fold the "water" up to cover the "land."

Noah's Ark

by Karen L. Spencer

This song is a lot of fun for children to sing to help them remember the story of Noah's Ark.

F F G G7
"No - ah, build an ark," God said. "Build it big and wide.
"Ga - ther up My an - i-mals, two of ev - 'ry kind, and

C7 C7 C7 F
I will send a flood to earth, but you'll be safe in - side." And the rain went
when the flood is o - ver I will send a spe - cial sign."

F F G G G7
drip drip drip, and the rain went drop drop drop, and the rain went

C C7 C7 1 F
drip drip drop drop drip drip drop drop. Will it ev - er stop?

2 F F F G
stop? At last the rain was o - ver and the earth be - gan to

G7 C C C7
dry. O - ver - head a rain - bow, God's pro - mise in the

F F F G
sky; and it did - n't drip drip drip, and it did - n't drop drop

G7 C C7
drop, and it did - n't drip drip drop drop drip drip drop drop. Shh - hh - hh - hh

C7 F
Lis - ten. The rain has stopped.

A Special Baby

Genesis 18:1–15; 21:1–3; 22:1–14

Abraham was a very old man. His wife, Sarah, was also old. She was too old to have children. This was a problem for both of them because they loved children and Abraham wanted sons and daughters and grandchildren.

God told Abraham he would become the father of many nations, even kings. But Abraham was 99 years old. Surely it was too late to have children!

A few days later, Abraham was sitting in front of his tent among some trees. He looked up and saw three men. Abraham was a courteous man. He didn't know who they were, but he bowed and said, *"If I have found favor in your eyes, my lord, do not pass your servant by. Let a little water be brought, and then you may all wash your feet and rest under this tree. Let me get you something to eat, so you can be refreshed . . ."* (Genesis 18:3–5)

He rushed into the tent to Sarah, his wife. He said, "Quick, get three measures of fine flour and knead it, and bake some bread." He then rushed out to his herd and found a calf, tender and good, and gave it to a servant who hurried to prepare it.

When the food was ready, Abraham brought it with curds and milk and gave it to the visitors. He stood by, under a tree, while they ate.

When they were done eating, they asked, "Where is Sarah, your wife?" By then, Abraham believed that the men were from God.

"She is in the tent," said Abraham.

"I will surely return to you about this time next year, and Sarah your wife will have a son," said one. (Genesis 18:10) The one who said this was actually the Lord! Sarah was listening just inside the tent. She laughed to herself because she was an old woman. Women can't have babies when they are old.

The Lord asked Abraham, *"Why did Sarah laugh . . . ? Is anything too hard for the Lord? I will return to you at the appointed time next year and Sarah will have a son."* (Genesis 18:13–14) As the Lord had promised, Sarah had a son, Isaac.

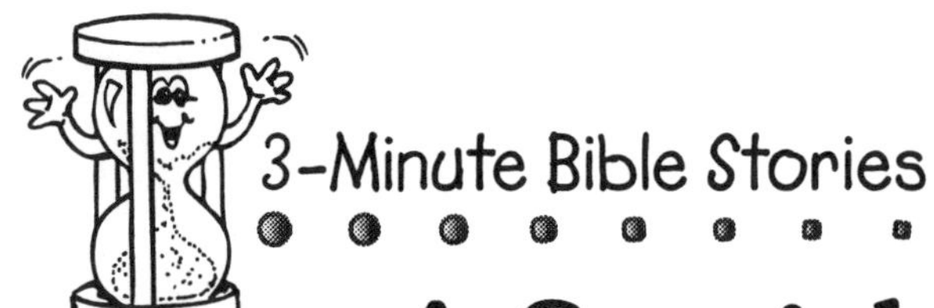

A Special Baby continued

Isaac was Abraham and Sarah's only child and they loved him dearly. God tested Abraham's love for Him by telling Abraham to take Isaac to the wilderness and offer him as a sacrifice.

Abraham cut some wood for the fire; then he called Isaac and two servants to go with him into the wilderness. Isaac said, "Father? *The fire and the wood are here . . . but where is the lamb for the burnt offering?"* (Genesis 22:7b)

"God will provide it," Abraham told him.

When they got to where they were going, Abraham laid out the wood for a fire. He picked up his knife. At that moment, he heard God's voice: "Abraham, Abraham."

"Here I am," Abraham said.

"Do not lay a hand on the boy," he said. "Do not do anything to him. Now I know that you fear God, because you have not withheld from me your son, your only son." (Genesis 22:12)

Abraham looked around. There behind him, he saw a ram caught by its horns in a thicket. Abraham took the ram and offered it as a burnt offering instead of his son.

Abraham named that place "The Lord Will Provide."

God spared Abraham's son that day. He also spared us by sending His own Son to die for our sins. He is a wonderful, loving God!

Promise Banner

This banner will help children remember that God keeps His promises.

Materials (per banner):

drinking straw
ruler
crayons
scissors
string or yarn
glue
one copy of the banner to the right

Directions:

1. Have the children color the banner and cut it out.
2. Cut a drinking straw to about 7" long for each child.
3. Help the children wrap the top of their banners around their straws and glue in place.
4. Cut an 18" piece of string for each child.
5. Help the children tie their strings through their straws for a hanger as illustrated.

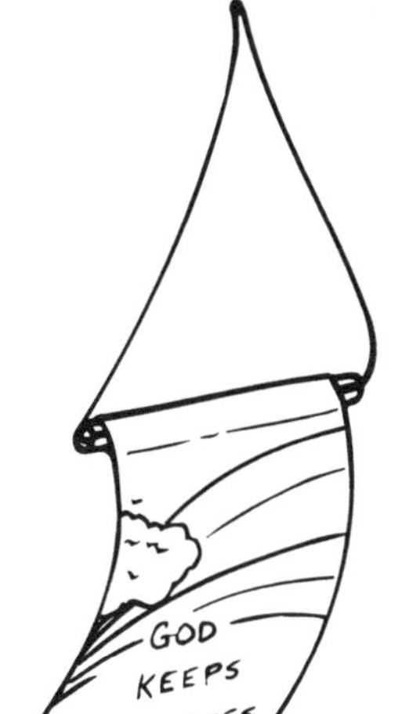

red
orange
yellow
blue
purple

GOD KEEPS HIS PROMISES

"Is anything too hard for the Lord?"
(Genesis 18:14a)

Picture This!

This picture will remind the children of Abraham's great love for the Lord.

Directions:

1. Make a copy of the picture below for each child.
2. Have the children color their pictures and cut them out on the bold lines.
3. Help them fanfold their pictures on the dotted lines.
4. Have the children stand their pictures on their edges. Then they look at their pictures from the left side, and then to see a different picture, from the right side.

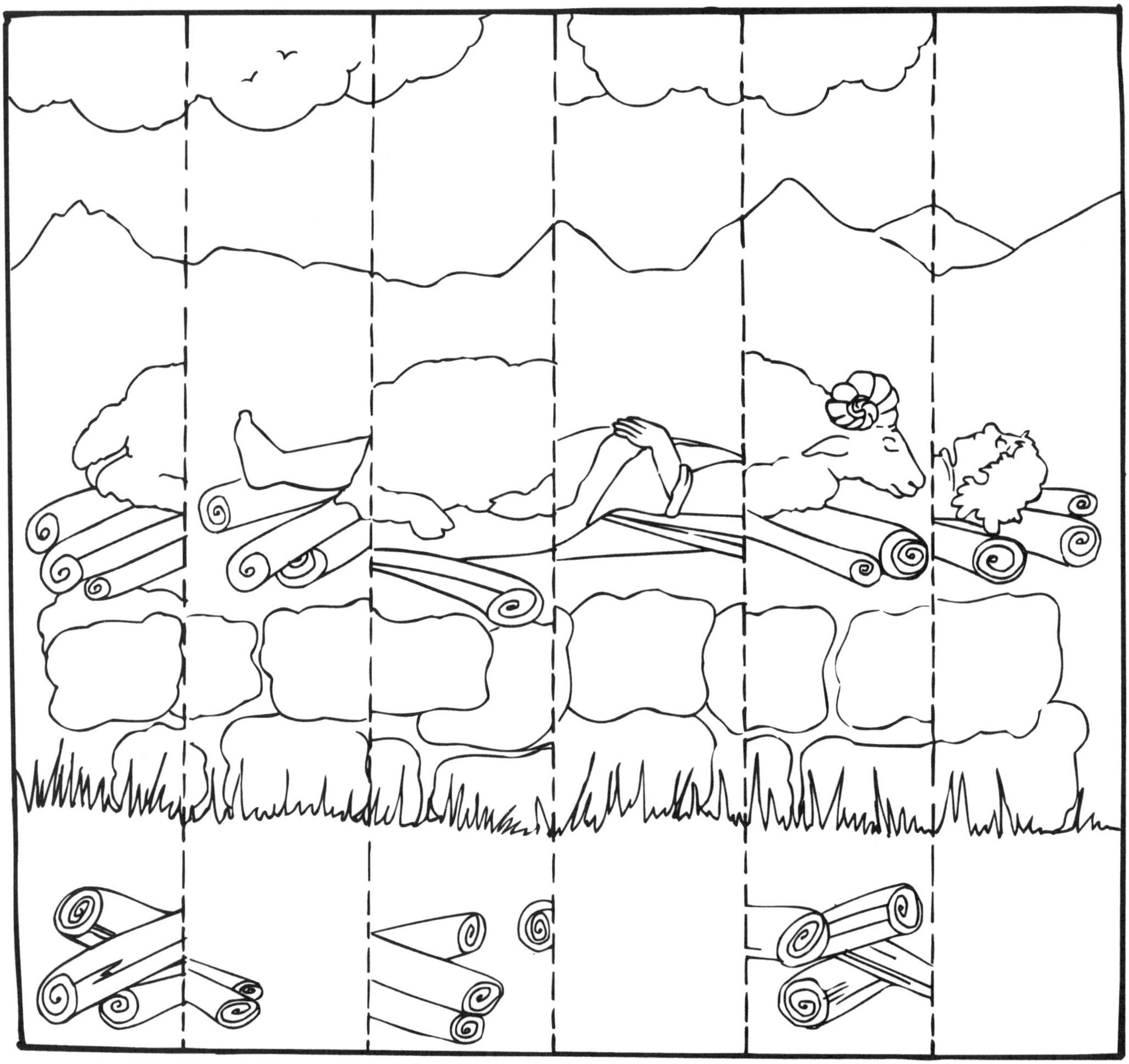

Jacob's Dream

Genesis 28:10–22

Jacob was the son of Isaac and Rebekah. He displeased his father and brother and was sent away to live with other relatives. It was a sad journey for Jacob. He stopped for the night in a stony place. He took one large stone, put it under his head for a pillow, and went to sleep. That must have been uncomfortable!

While he was asleep, Jacob had a wonderful dream. Jacob dreamed that there was a stairway reaching from the ground where he lay all the way up to heaven. He dreamed that he saw angels on the stairway going up and down. They were coming and going to do the will of God.

At the top of the stairway in Jacob's dream stood the Lord God Himself. God spoke to Jacob. He promised that He would give Jacob the land where he was sleeping. God also told him that he would have many children and grandchildren to live in that land. Finally, God spoke a blessing for all Jacob's people.

When he woke up, Jacob remembered his dream with wonder and awe. He was amazed at all that God had promised. He said, "Surely God is here, and I didn't realize it."

Because God had promised him so much, Jacob wanted to do something special for God. He took the stone that he had used for a pillow and set it up on end. He poured oil on it as if it were an altar and he was making a special offering.

Jacob's Dream continued

He said, "This place must be the house of God, and the very gate of heaven." He called the place Bethel, which means "the house of God," as a reminder that this was the place where he had dreamed a wonderful dream.

After he poured the oil on the altar stone, Jacob made a vow. He promised that if God would protect him on the journey he was taking, the Lord would always be the God of Jacob. Jacob would worship Him and give God His proper share of everything he ever had.

Then Jacob went on his way. He came at last to the home of Laban, his uncle. For many years, he worked for Laban, and Jacob married while he was there. But he never forgot seeing the angels going up and down on the stairway from heaven to earth.

Jacob's Dream Flannelboard

This flannelboard is the perfect way for each child to retell the story of "Jacob's Dream."

Materials:
copies of patterns on this page, crayons, scissors, sandpaper, flannel, cardboard, glue

Directions:
Make a copy of the patterns for each child. Instruct the children to color them and cut them out. They can glue small sandpaper squares to the back of each pattern. Have each child glue flannel to a piece of cardboard to create a flannelboard. The children can use the patterns to retell the story.

A Sure Sign

(Sing to the tune of "London Bridge" while using appropriate hand motions.)

Angel feet walked up and down,
Up and down, up and down.
Angel feet walked up and down,
In Jacob's dream.

(Raise and lower arms while wiggling fingers during first three lines.)

(Fold hands, close eyes, and rest face sideways on hands.)

Above the stairway stood the Lord,
Stood the Lord, stood the Lord.
Above the stairway stood the Lord,
In Jacob's dream.

(Lift arms and look up during first three lines.)

(Fold hands, close eyes, and rest face sideways on hands.)

Jacob woke and set the stone,
Set the stone, set the stone.
Jacob woke and set the stone,
Where he had dreamed.

(Bend over, lift, and set stone during first three lines.)

(Fold hands, close eyes, and rest face sideways on hands.)

"This shall be a sign," he said.
"Sign," he said, "Sign," he said.
"This shall be a sign," he said,
"That God was here!"

(Point to stone during first three lines.)

(Lift arms and face, then point down on last word.)

Repeat stanza 1.

Jacob Went

If you do not have a piano or time to practice a song, try clapping out the rhythm of these simple verses as children chant them. The words may also be sung to the tune of "Jack and Jill" or recited as a jump rope rhyme.

Jacob went
Where he was sent,
And found a wife to marry.

On a stone
He slept alone,
But dreamed he saw a stairway.

Joseph and His Brothers

Genesis 37; 42; 45

A long time ago in Israel, there were 12 brothers. They were the sons of a man named Jacob. They all herded their father's sheep.

One boy's name was Joseph. Jacob loved Joseph very much and gave him a fancy coat of many colors. This made his brothers very angry.

Joseph was a dreamer. His brothers didn't like him because he told them about his dreams. They knew their father loved Joseph best, and they were jealous of him.

One day, the brothers plotted to kill Joseph. One brother who didn't want to kill him said, "Let's just throw him in this hole and leave him here." He planned to come back later and take Joseph out of the hole.

The brothers threw Joseph into the hole, then sat down to eat lunch.

While they were eating, a caravan of Ishmaelites came by. One brother suggested that selling Joseph to the Ishmaelites would be a good way to get rid of him. So they sold Joseph to the men in the caravan.

"Let's kill a goat and put its blood on Joseph's coat," said the brothers. "We can tell Father a wild animal killed him." Jacob was very sad when he was told that his beloved son Joseph had been killed.

Joseph was taken to Egypt and sold into slavery. Years passed and with God's help, he worked his way out of slavery. He even became a very important man in the Egyptian court.

A famine hit the land of Israel. Jacob sent his sons to Egypt to try to buy food. When the brothers arrived in Egypt, they had to deal with an important man in Pharaoh's court—Joseph! Although Joseph recognized his brothers, they did not recognize him.

The brothers made several trips to Egypt to buy food, but Joseph did not tell them who he was. Finally one day, he sent his servants from the room and told his brothers, "I am your brother, Joseph!" He told them that he forgave them because it was God's plan that he should be in Egypt.

Have the children memorize the Bible verse below. See if they agree with the verse and explain why.

Now Israel loved Joseph more than any of his other sons. (Genesis 37:3a)

So Jealous

Ask children if they enjoy receiving gifts from their parents. Ask how they would feel if a brother or sister were given a beautiful new coat but they did not get one. Would they be jealous? How does God want us to respond when we have jealous feelings? Explain that Joseph's brothers were jealous of him.

A Special Robe

This activity is fun for children to do to create their very own beautiful coat for Joseph.

Materials:
copies of the patterns on this page, scissors, crayons, glue, trims like cloth, rickrack, sequins, etc.

Directions:
Let the children cut out the patterns and use the materials to decorate their robes. Then they can glue their robes on their patterns of Joseph.

Puzzle Fun

This puzzle is a nice reminder of God's greatness for the children. Discuss with the children how Joseph being sold to the merchants ended up being a good thing.

GOD WORKS ALL THINGS OUT FOR HIS GOOD.

Materials:
crayons
scissors
glue
copies of the circle pattern on this page
thin cardboard (such as a cereal box)

Directions:

1. Give each child a circle pattern. Have the children color their circle patterns.
2. Help each child spread an even layer of glue on a piece of cardboard slightly larger than the circle. They lay their circles on the cardboard and press them down evenly and firmly.
3. When dry, have the children cut out their circles along the outer edge. Then they cut apart on the dotted lines to make puzzles.
4. When not using the puzzles, have the children store the pieces in an envelope.

Where Is Joseph?

This song may be sung in unison or by two groups, one asking the questions and the other answering. Sing it to the tune of "Frère Jacques."

Where is Joseph? Where is Joseph?
In the well. In the well.
Did you take his coat off?
His many-colored coat off?
Here's his coat. Here's his coat.

Where is Joseph? Where is Joseph?
He's not there. He's not there.
He is sold to Egypt,
To be a slave in Egypt.
Here's his coat. Here's his coat.

Where is Joseph? Where is Joseph?
He is gone. He is gone.
We will tell our father
A lion killed our brother.
Here's his coat. Here's his coat.

Where is Joseph? Where is Joseph?
Jacob weeps. Jacob weeps.
We are so ashamed that
We only tell our father,
"Here's his coat. Here's his coat."

Joseph Finds His Brothers

Have all but two children in the group join hands, standing far apart to represent a flock of sheep. One of the children not in the group should be Joseph; the other should be a brother. The brother makes himself hard to find by going through the "sheep" toward the center of the circle, then out again, alternating in and out between "sheep" until he returns to his starting place.

"Joseph" must follow in and out the same way, trying to catch his brother. When he does tag him, the brother becomes Joseph, and a new brother is chosen. If he is unsuccessful, both Joseph and his brother become sheep, and new contestants try.

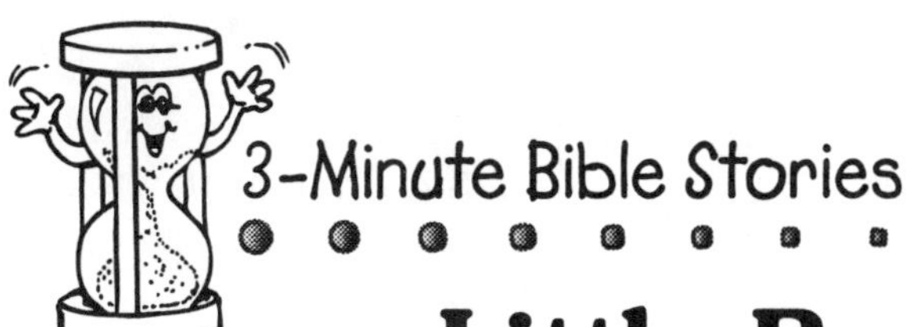

Little Boat in the Reeds

Exodus 2:1–10

Back in the days when the Israelites were slaves in Egypt, the rulers of Egypt were called pharaohs. One of the pharaohs hated the Israelites so much, he gave an order that all their boy babies were to be thrown into the Nile River to drown.

One Israelite woman who had a baby boy could not bear to see her child hurt, so she hid him until he was three months old. She worried that he would be found and killed. She would also be punished, probably with death, if Pharaoh's soldiers found her baby.

One day, she made a little boat like a basket. Pharaoh had said to put the boy babies into the Nile, and she would—in a little boat! She placed the little boat, containing her baby, into the river among the reeds.

When Pharaoh's daughter went down to the river with her handmaidens, she saw the basket-boat and sent one of her handmaidens to get it. When she saw the Israelite baby, she decided to keep him for her own. She named him Moses.

Moses was treated well by the daughter of Pharaoh and was an important person in Pharaoh's household. He grew up in Egypt.

The Baby's Boat

What a fun way to reinforce the story of baby Moses!

Materials:
copies of the patterns shown, crayons, scissors, glue

Directions:

1. Have the children color the fronts and backs of the patterns and cut them out on the bold lines.
2. Tell them to fold the patterns on the dotted lines.
3. Help them apply glue to tabs and fasten to form a basket-boat.
4. The children can lay their babies in their baskets.

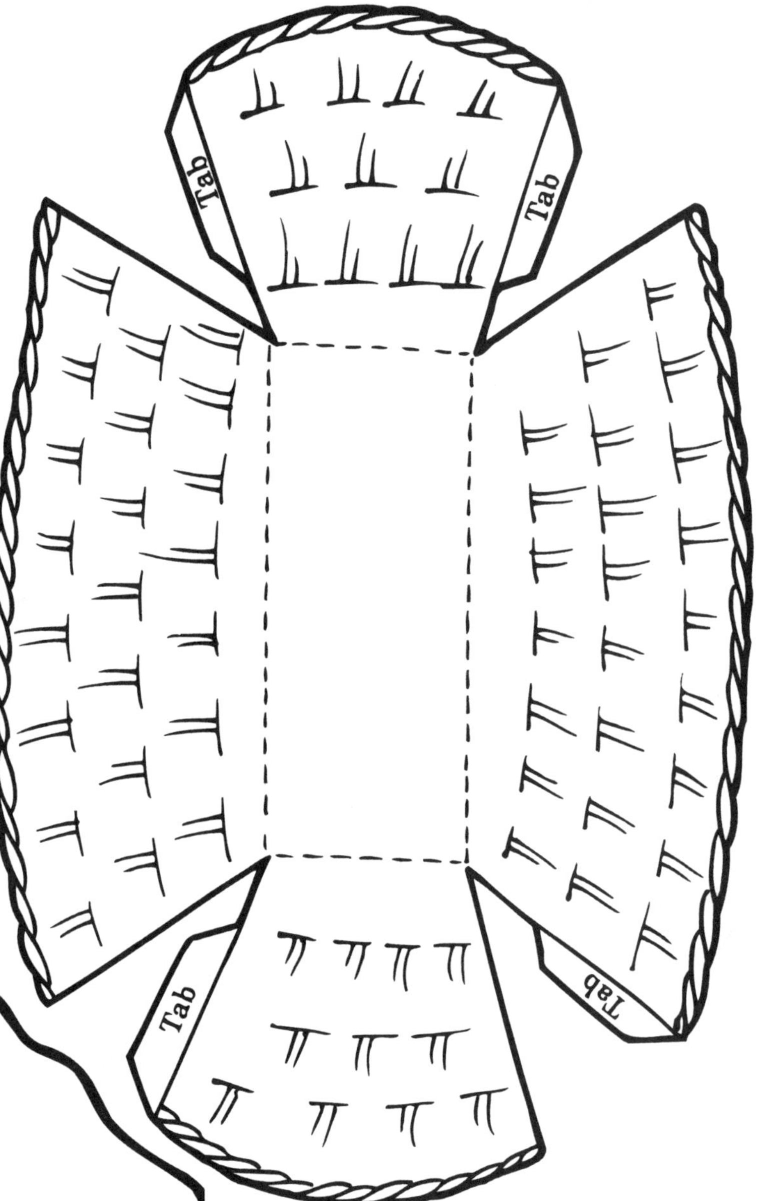

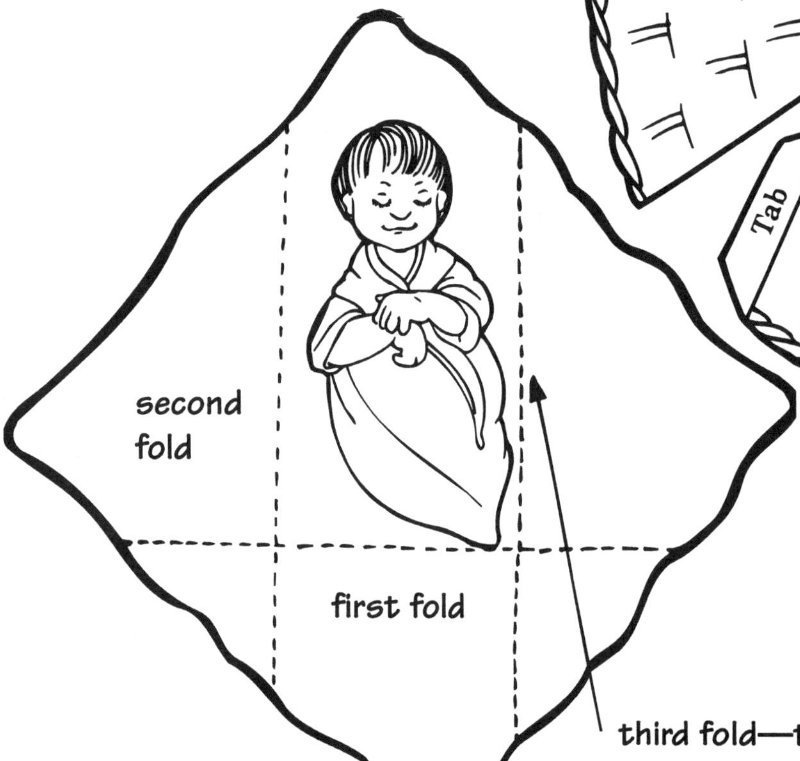

"Garden of God's Love" Bulletin Board

Moses was a very special baby. God chose him to one day lead the people of Israel. Like Moses, each one of us is also special in God's eyes. Make a bulletin board entitled "Garden of God's Love."

Materials:

light brown craft or wrapping paper
construction paper: red, blue, purple, white, yellow, green
patterns (page 36) glue
green pipe cleaners scissors
crayons stapler (optional)

Directions:

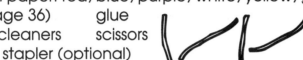

1. Trace each child's hand on a piece of construction paper (any color but green) and cut it out. (Some children's fingers may be spread out, others may be held closely together to make different looking flowers. Right or left hands may be traced.)
2. To make some flowers different, fold the thumb and baby finger cutouts inward and glue in place.
3. Glue or staple the handprints to a bulletin board which you have covered with brown paper.
4. Use green construction paper or green pipe cleaners to make flower stems (see patterns on page 36). Note: If using pipe cleaners, use only the leaves pattern on page 36. Glue the stems under the flowers. Have the children write their names next to their flowers using crayons.
5. Point out to the children that each flower is different, yet very special, just like each of us is special to God.

Patterns

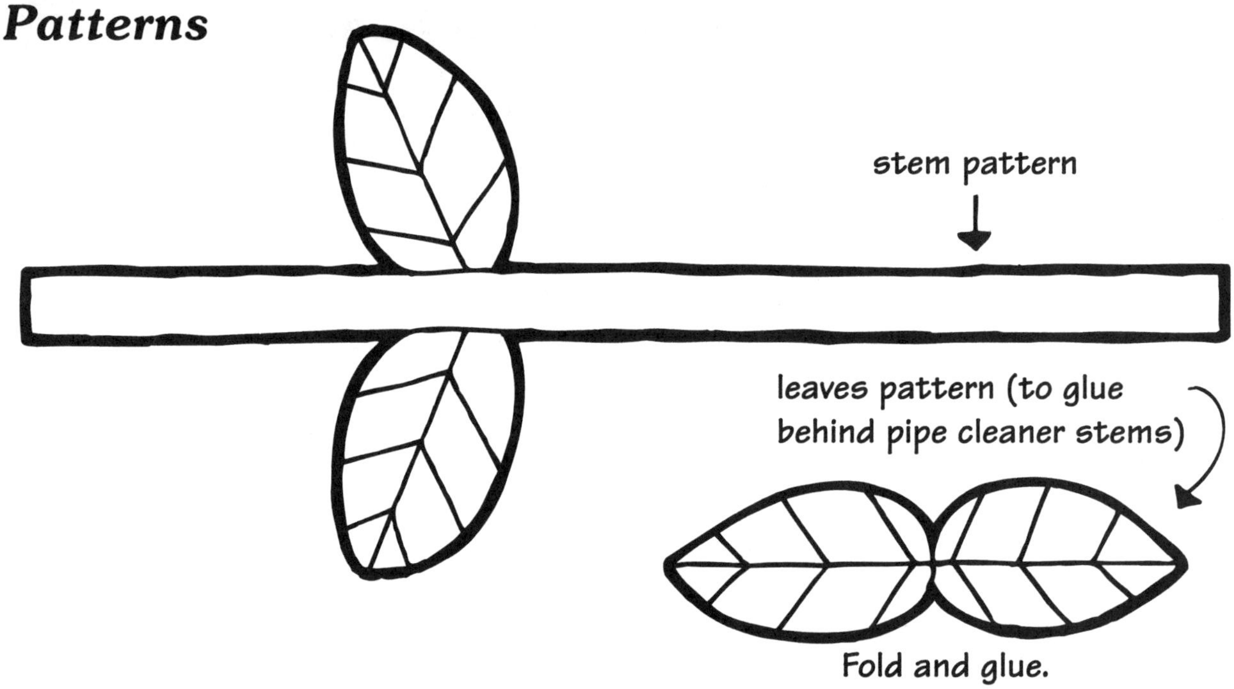

stem pattern

leaves pattern (to glue behind pipe cleaner stems)

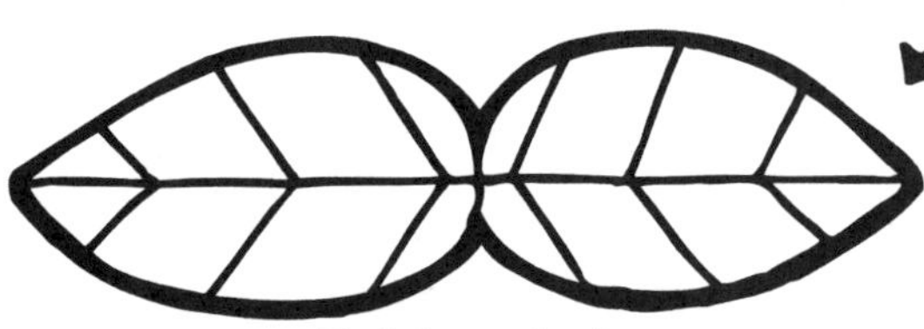

Fold and glue.

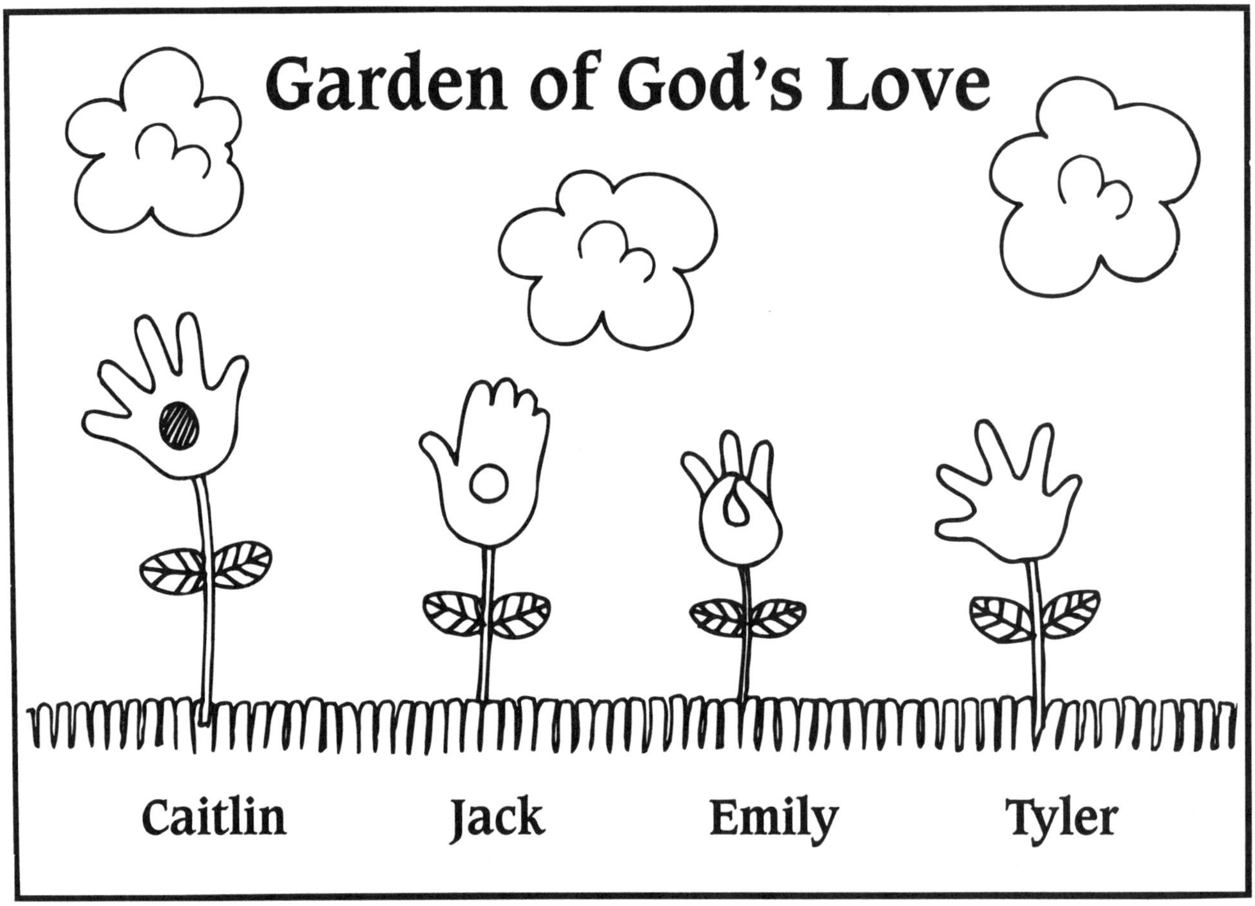

Garden of God's Love

Caitlin Jack Emily Tyler

God's Garden of Love

by Karen L. Spencer

The children will learn all about God's "Garden of Love" when they sing this song.

C C C

1. God takes a ti - ny seed and then He plants it with care.___ He_____
2. I_____ am a tu - lip and I am a rose.___________
3. My_____ co - lor is pur - ple;_____ my pet - als are blue.___________
4. When you're feel - ing down, you're not as good as the rest.___ When you

G7 G7 C

o - pens up His heart and gives, each one a share.___ He makes them grow big - ger and He
I_____ am a dai - sy 'cuz that's how it goes.____ I_____ am a vio - let as____
I am kind of crook-ed 'cuz that's how I grew.____ All of us are diff-'rent; that's
think that be - ing some-thing else is prob - ab - ly best.____ Think___ what a drag___ the_____

C7 F G G7 C

lets them grow tall.___ He cares____ for them e - qual - ly, one and all.___
shy as can be.___ But that's____ o - kay______ 'cuz God made me.___
plain_____ to see.___ 'Cuz God_____ made____ us___ so spe - cial - ly.____
world____ would be___ if flow - ers looked a - like___ ex - act - ly.__________

Chorus

C C C

Oh we're all______ spe - cial flow - ers in God's gar - den of love.____ We're
(Last time)
Do do do do do do do do do do do do do do_____ do

G G7 C

all spe - cial flow - ers in God's gar - den of love.____.
do do do do do do do do do do do.______

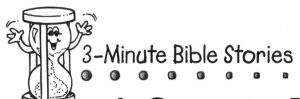

A Strange Way to Meet God

Exodus 3:1–4:21

When Moses grew to be a man, he got in trouble in Egypt. He saw an Egyptian beating an Israelite. He was so angry that he killed the Egyptian. He ran away to the land of Midian to hide from the soldiers who would be looking for him.

Moses married and began tending the flocks of his father-in-law. One day, Moses was walking along when a bush nearby burst into flames. The bush was not burned but the flames kept burning. This was an unusual sight, so he decided to take a closer look.

As he walked nearer, he heard a voice. "Moses! Moses!" The voice was coming from the bush.

"Here I am," said Moses.

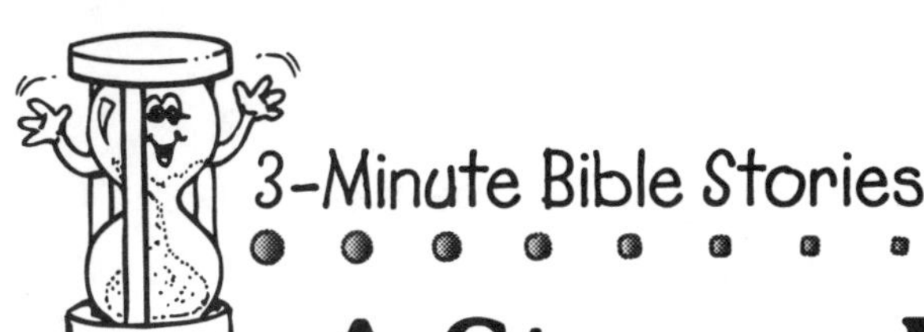

A Strange Way . . . continued

"Do not come any closer . . . Take off your sandals, for the place where you are standing is holy ground." (Exodus 3:5) It was the voice of God! He said, *"I am the God of your father, the God of Abraham, the God of Isaac and the God of Jacob."* (Exodus 3:6) Moses took off his sandals and hid his face. He was afraid to look at God.

God said, *"I have indeed seen the misery of my people in Egypt. I have heard them crying out because of their slave drivers, and I am concerned about their suffering. So I have come down to rescue them from the hand of the Egyptians and to bring them out of that land into a good and spacious land, a land flowing with milk and honey . . . I am sending you to Pharaoh to bring my people the Israelites out of Egypt."* (Exodus 3:7–10)

"Why do you want me to go to Pharaoh and bring the Israelites out of Egypt?" Moses asked.

"I will be with you," said God. *"And this will be the sign to you that it is I who have sent you: When you have brought the people out of Egypt, you will worship God on this mountain."* (Exodus 3:12)

They talked for a while; then Moses worried aloud, "Oh Lord, I am slow of speech and tongue."

"Go," said God. "I will help you speak and will teach you what to say. What about your brother, Aaron? He is already on his way to meet you and his heart will be glad when he sees you. You shall speak to him and put words in his mouth; I will help both of you speak. It will be as if he were your mouth and as if you were God to him." Then God told Moses to take a staff in his hand so he could perform miraculous signs with it.

The Burning Bush

This burning bush will help remind the children of God's appearance to Moses.

Materials:
copies of the patterns shown, crayons, scissors, hole punch, brad fasteners

Directions:

1. Have the children color the bushes. Then they should color their wheels using the color chart below.
2. Tell the children to cut out the patterns on the bold lines.
3. Help the children use a hole punch to punch out all the black circles on their bushes.

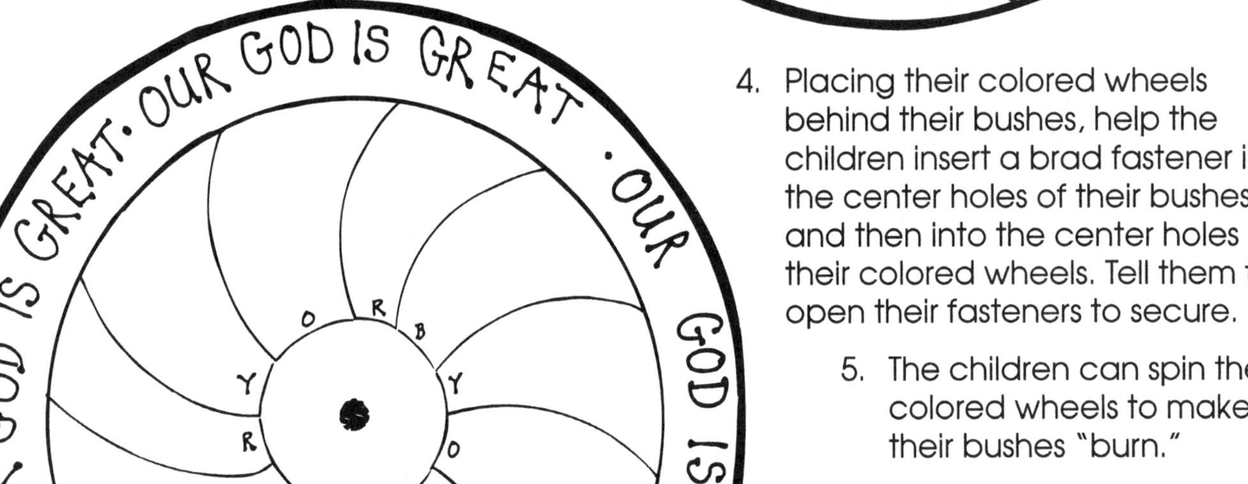

4. Placing their colored wheels behind their bushes, help the children insert a brad fastener in the center holes of their bushes and then into the center holes of their colored wheels. Tell them to open their fasteners to secure.
5. The children can spin their colored wheels to make their bushes "burn."

Y—yellow
O—orange
R—red
B—brown

The Plagues

Exodus 7:14–12:41

Moses and his brother, Aaron, were chosen by God to lead the Israelites out of Egypt and into the Promised Land. But the ruler of Egypt was stubborn. He wanted the Israelites to stay in Egypt and be his slaves.

"Let my people go!" demanded Moses to Pharaoh. "The Lord will punish you and your people if you do not let the Israelites leave."

The Pharaoh shook his head, "No!"

God told Aaron to stretch out his hand over the waters of Egypt—over all the streams, canals, ponds, and lakes. When Moses and Aaron did as the Lord had commanded, the waters turned to blood! All the fish died, and the Egyptians could not drink.

But Pharaoh did not love God and did not want to obey Him. "I will not let these people of Israel go. I will make them work harder. We will beat them until they die!" he said.

God told Aaron to stretch out his rod over the rivers and ponds. This time, frogs came up and covered the land. They hopped around in houses and on people. Thousands and thousands of frogs were leaping through the kingdom. At last, Pharaoh screamed, "I promise to let the people go if your God will take away the frogs!" But when God took away the frogs, Pharaoh did not keep his promise.

God sent another plague to Egypt. Tiny, stinging bugs called gnats crawled from the dust onto the animals and people, biting them until the people cried to Pharaoh to let the Israelites go. Again, Pharaoh promised to let the people go if the gnats were taken away. But again, he broke his promise.

The next time, the Lord sent a plague of flies that swarmed through the Egyptian palace. Then He sent a terrible disease that killed all the cattle that belonged to the Egyptians. Pharaoh still refused to let God's people go.

The Lord said to Moses, "Toss handfuls of soot into the air." Moses did, and horrible, painful sores broke out on all the Egyptian people and their animals.

A hailstorm, locusts, and a plague of darkness also came on the land. But Pharaoh still refused to let the people of Israel go.

The Lord sent one more plague. All the first-born male children in Egypt died, but not one of the Israelites was harmed. What a sad morning when the Egyptians awoke. Crying was heard all across the land. Pharaoh's oldest son lay dead. "Leave," wailed Pharaoh. "Take these Israelites from my sight."

The Israelites left the land of Egypt. Hundreds of thousands of God's people walked together, following Moses and Aaron. Israelites had been in Egypt for 430 years. Now God was keeping His promise, leading His people to the Promised Land.

Plague Bingo

This game is fun for the children to play and helps them learn the plagues that God sent to the Egyptians.

Directions:

Make several copies of the plague pictures on page 43 and the bingo card below. Cut apart and keep one set of plague pictures separate in an envelope. Cut out the pictures and glue them on the bingo cards in different orders. (The order of pictures on each card should be different.)

Give each child a bingo card and some buttons, small crackers, or cereal for markers. Using the pictures in the envelope, choose one and call it out for the group. Each child puts a marker on that picture. When a child gets three markers in a row—across, down, or diagonally—have him or her stand up and say, "Let my people go!"

"Plague Bingo" Patterns

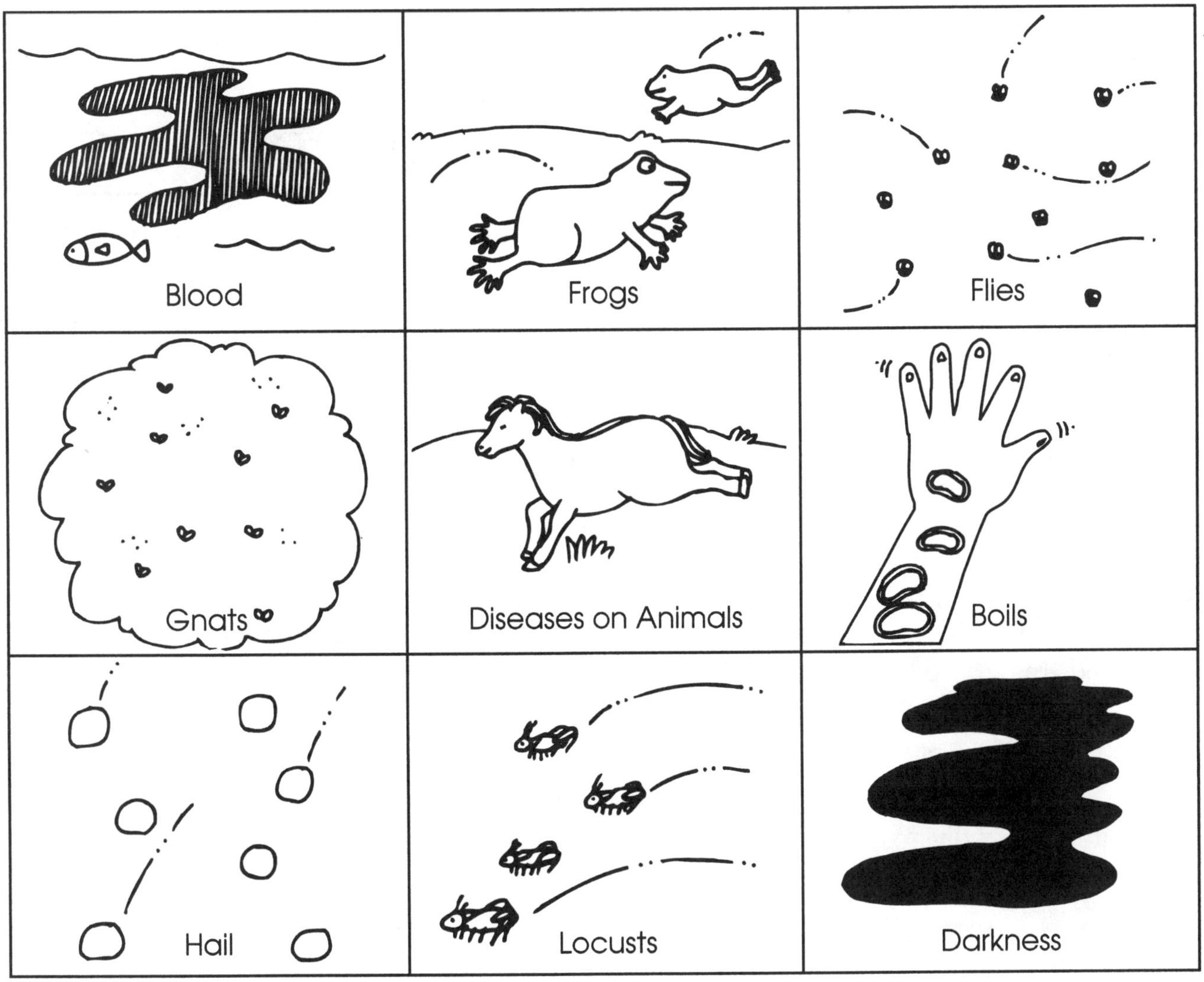

Blood	Frogs	Flies
Gnats	Diseases on Animals	Boils
Hail	Locusts	Darkness

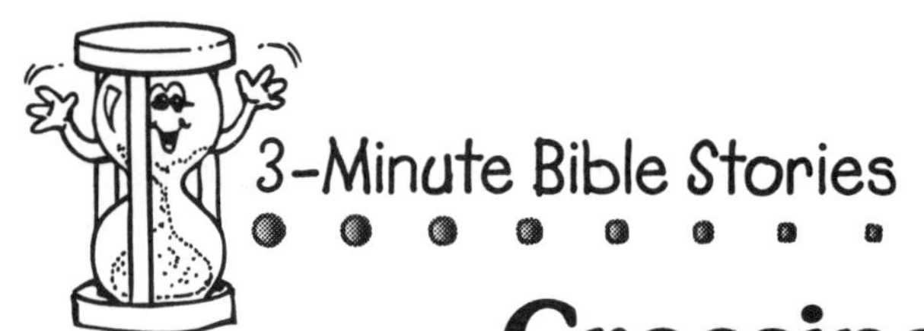

Crossing the Red Sea

Exodus 13:17–14:31

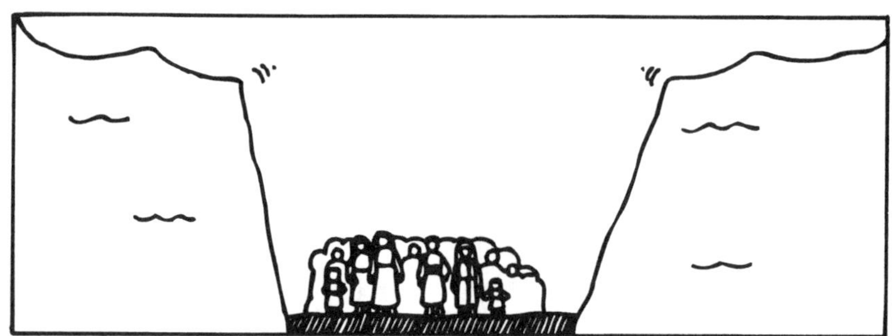

When Pharaoh finally agreed to let them go, the Israelites packed a few belongings and hurried away. Through the desert they walked, in search of the free land God had promised them. By day, the Lord went ahead of them in a pillar of cloud and by night in a pillar of fire. Neither the pillar of cloud nor the pillar of fire left its place in front of the people.

Pharaoh soon realized that he should not have let Moses and Aaron lead their people away. With all the Israelites gone, there was no one to work for him. He gathered his army and marched off to find the Israelites.

God led His people to the edge of the Red Sea to camp for the night. When the Israelites saw the Egyptian soldiers coming after them, they cried out, "Why did you bring us out of Egypt, Moses? It would have been better for us to serve Pharaoh than to die in the desert."

Moses called to his people, "Do not be afraid. The Lord will fight for you; just be still and believe."

The Lord told Moses, "Raise your staff and stretch out your hand over the sea." When Moses did this, the pillar of cloud moved from the front and stood behind them, coming between the armies of Egypt and Israel. All night, the cloud brought darkness to Egypt's side and light to Israel's side.

All that night, the Lord drove the sea back with a strong wind, until it became dry land. The waters were divided, and the Israelites walked through the sea on dry ground, with a wall of water on their right and on their left.

The next morning, the Egyptians saw how the seas had parted. They drove their chariots after the Israelites. Then the Lord said to Moses, "Stretch out your hand over the sea so that the waters will flow back over the Egyptians and their chariots and horsemen."

Moses stretched out his hand over the sea, and at daybreak, the sea went back to its place. The water covered all the chariots and horsemen, the whole army of Pharaoh. Not one of them was left alive. Not one of the Israelites was harmed. The Lord had saved Israel from the hands of the Egyptians.

When the Israelites saw the great power the Lord had shown against the Egyptians, the people feared the Lord and put their trust in Him and in Moses.

Red Sea Recipes

Today, many Jewish people still celebrate Passover. The tradition began 3,000 years ago when the Israelites were forced to flee from Egypt. While they were getting ready for their trip, they didn't have enough time to wait for the yeast bread to rise. So they quickly baked unleavened bread to take with them.

Make unleavened bread for a snack and serve it with Red Sea Punch (below).

Unleavened Bread

Ingredients:

2 cups whole wheat flour
½ tsp. salt
½ to ¾ cup warm water
griddle
spoon
mixing bowl

Directions:

1. Blend flour and salt in mixing bowl.
2. Add water until dough is evenly moist and sticks together.
3. Knead on floured surface. At first, the dough will be crumbly, but after kneading for about 5 minutes, it will become smooth.
4. Divide dough in half and roll out on a floured surface. Dough should be about ⅛" thick and slightly smaller than the griddle on which it will be cooked.
5. Lightly flour the griddle and place over low heat.
6. Place the dough on the griddle and cook 15–18 minutes on each side. Bread is done when the outside is crisp but the inside is still slightly soft.

Red Sea Punch

Ingredients:

2 quarts cranberry juice cocktail, chilled
1 can (6 oz.) frozen pink lemonade concentrate, thawed
1 quart sparkling water, chilled

Directions:

Mix cranberry juice cocktail and lemonade concentrate in a large punch bowl. Just before serving, stir in sparkling water.

Fighting for Freedom

(Sing to the tune of "Itsy Bitsy Spider.")

Divide the class into three groups. One group should join hands in a circle to be the Red Sea; one group should form a line to be the Israelites with Moses leading them; the third group should be Egyptians. (If the class is small, one child may represent the Israelites and one the Egyptians. This will leave the rest of the class to represent the Red Sea which should surround the Egyptians.)

During the first two stanzas, the Israelites march around the room and up to the Red Sea. When Moses reaches out his arm, the Red Sea circle divides into two parallel lines to let the Israelites through. When the Egyptians approach, the lines reform the circle, surrounding them.

The Israelites left Egypt's land.
They wanted to be free.

Great Moses led them
Onward to the sea.

There God was with them.
And kept them safe from harm.

For Moses did what God had said,
And he stretched out his arm.

The Red Sea opened wide and dry
To let God's people through:

Men, women, children,
Sheep, and cattle, too.

Then came the Egyptians
With horses wild and fast.

But the Red Sea closed its waves again
And would not let them past.

Leaving Egypt

The Israelites had to go slowly as they left Egypt because they were taking their sheep and cows with them. Choose a child to be Moses. He (or she) is the shepherd. The rest of the children bend or squat and grasp their ankles with their hands, thus representing sheep. Moses leads the sheep as they try to reach the Red Sea (the opposite side of the room). The first sheep who reaches the other side of the room without losing hold of his or her ankles becomes the new Moses. All others return to the starting line and a new race begins. This time, the children may grasp their knees (because cows are taller than sheep) as they try to reach the Red Sea.

Choral Reading *(Based on Psalm 23)*

God led His people out of Egypt, across the Red Sea, and through the desert. He gave them rules to keep them happy. He watched over them and cared for them like a shepherd cares for his sheep.

Copy this choral reading for each child. Have the class read it together.

Girls: **The Lord is my shepherd.**
Boys: **He gives me all I need.**
All: **The Lord takes good care of me.**

Girls: **The Lord is my shepherd.**
Boys: **He walks by my side.**
All: **The Lord takes good care of me.**

Girls: **The Lord is my shepherd.**
Boys: **I shall not fear.**
All: **The Lord takes good care of me.**

Girls: **The Lord is my shepherd.**
Boys: **He'll always be near.**
All: **The Lord takes good care of me.**

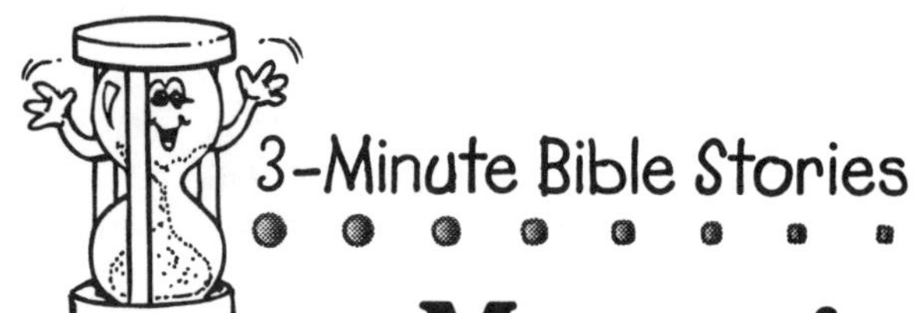

Manna in the Wilderness

Exodus 16:14–35

After the Israelites had crossed the Red Sea, they wandered in the desert for a long time. They ate all the bread and used the flour they had brought with them. They got tired of the food they had and forgot that they had promised to trust God. Every day, they complained to Moses. At last, Moses took his problem to God. He asked what to do about the people's complaining.

God said to Moses, "I will send down food as if it were raining! Have each person pick up enough to eat for just one day. The next morning, more food will rain down. On the sixth day, everyone is to pick up enough for two days. They are not to work on the Sabbath, so no food will come down on that day. Let them hear and obey."

The next morning when people looked out of their tents, they saw a heavy dew on the ground. After that dried up, there was a thin layer of little things that looked like snowflakes on the ground.

"What is that?" people asked. They had never seen anything like it before.

"That is the food the Lord has sent," Moses told them. It looked like small, white seeds. When they put some in their mouths, it was sweet, like honey-flavored crackers. They called it manna.

Moses told the people what God had said. They were to pick up all they would need for one day but not keep any overnight. When they had picked up all they needed, the rest melted away.

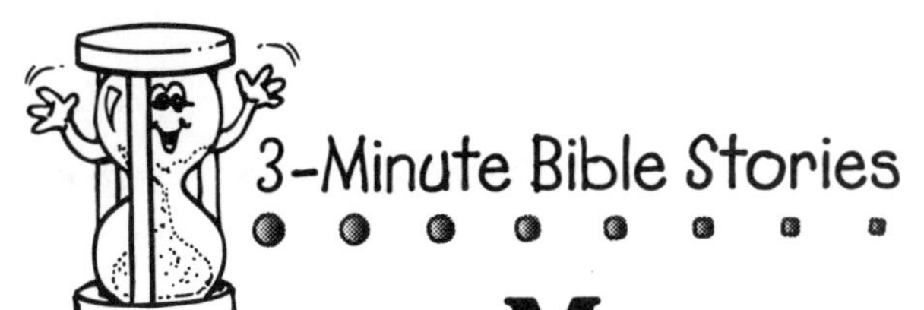

Manna . . . continued

Some people listened and did as Moses said, but some did not. Some people picked up too much that first day. They thought they would have enough left over so that they would not have to pick up any the next day. When they got up the next morning, they found that the leftover manna had spoiled. It smelled terrible, and there were ugly little worms crawling in it.

Then came the sixth day, and most people picked up twice as much. Moses said that was right because the next day was the Sabbath. They were not to work on the Sabbath.

Again, some people didn't pay attention. In spite of what Moses had told them, they did not gather extra for the Sabbath. They went out for manna on the morning of the Sabbath, but there was nothing there. Those people had to go hungry that day.

At last, the Israelites learned to do as God told them. For 40 years, God sent them manna. They ate it every day until they arrived in the land God had promised them.

Tasting Manna

Have the children put their heads down with their eyes closed to simulate night. While they are not looking, spread a sheet on the floor and cover it with Cheerios™ or another children's cereal.

Wake the children for "morning" and give each a small paper cup to be filled with the day's ration. (They may eat what they want after each one has filled a cup, but not while they are picking up the manna.)

Have You Heard?

This song may be sung to the tune of "Did You Ever See a Lassie?" You may want to let children pretend to gather manna as they sing.

Have you heard about the manna,
The manna, the manna?
Have you heard about the manna
In God's wilderness?

He sent it to the hungry,
Like dewdrops of sweetness.
Have you heard about the manna
In God's wilderness?

Let us gather up the manna,
The manna, the manna.
Let us gather up the manna
God gives us today.

We'll eat it and thank Him
For sending it to us.
Let us gather up the manna
God gives us today.

God's Rules

Exodus 20

Moses had led the Israelite people out of Egyptian slavery. Now they were camped at Mount Sinai. God told Moses to meet Him at the top of the mountain. Moses obeyed, and heard these commands from God:

1. The people were to have no other gods but Him.
2. They were not to make any idols to worship because God was a jealous God.
3. The people were not to use God's name in a bad way.
4. They were to keep the Sabbath day holy because it was the day God rested after creating the world.
5. God expected the people to honor their mothers and fathers. If they would do this, they would live long lives.
6. God's people should not murder.
7. He did not want them to commit adultery.
8. He did not want them to steal.
9. They should not tell lies about their neighbors.
10. They should not covet anything belonging to their neighbors.

All God's rules were written on stone tablets to be kept in a safe place from that day forward.

Have the children memorize this Bible verse to say before they recite one, several, or all of the Ten Commandments:

And God spoke all these words: (Exodus 20:1)

Introduction

Before class, cut out fifteen 2" x 8" strips of paper and have two sheets of posterboard ready. On ten strips, print the commandments as shown. Print the following on the five remaining strips: *You shall not eat candy on Sunday; You shall not talk loudly in church; You shall not drink sodas; You shall take care of your pets; You shall not ride your bike at night.* Share these with the children and lay them out on the table.

Ask the children to share some of the rules they have to obey each day at home, school, or in the community. Explain that God gave His people some special rules to live by. Ask children to read the rules on the strips. As they listen carefully to the story, have them raise their hands if they hear their rules mentioned.

When a child says he or she hears a rule, let him or her take the strip and tape it to a sheet of posterboard. Place five commandments on each sheet. Have children read the five remaining rules and discuss why they are not from God.

You shall have no other gods before me.

You shall not make for yourself an idol.

You shall not misuse the name of the Lord your God.

Remember the Sabbath day by keeping it holy.

Honor your father and your mother.

You shall not murder.

You shall not commit adultery.

You shall not steal.

You shall not give false testimony.

You shall not covet.

Ten Commandments Craft

The children will love creating their own stone tablets of rules.

Materials:
clay
paper
glue
copies of the commandments patterns above

Directions:
Provide each child with enough clay to form two 2" x 4" stone tablets. Give each child a copy of the commandments patterns. Have the children glue the patterns on the clay.

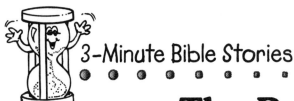

The Promised Land

Numbers 13:1–2, 17–33; 14:1–3, 26–30

When the Israelites had come near to the land that God had promised them, the Lord told Moses to send some men ahead to explore the country. Moses appointed 12 men, one from each tribe, to go see what the Promised Land was like.

Moses told the 12 men to find out if there were many people and if they were big or little. He told them to find out if the cities had high walls around them. "Find out if the ground is good," he said. He even told them to bring back some of the fruit of the land if they could.

The 12 men went into the land. They looked at the land and the cities and the people. After 40 days, they came back to share what they had seen. They even brought back a bunch of grapes so big that two men had to carry it on a pole between them.

The men all said it was a rich land, "flowing with milk and honey." ("Flowing with milk and honey" were the words people used in those days to mean that there were a lot of good things to eat and drink there.)

But 10 of the men were afraid of this new land. They said there were big cities with high walls around them and the people were like giants! "The men were so big," they said, "that we seemed like grasshoppers!"

The Promised Land continued

Two of the men did not agree with the others. Caleb and Joshua were not afraid. They said, "Let's do what the Lord wants us to. The Lord is with us. We can do what He tells us." Even though there were big walled cities, Caleb and Joshua were sure God would help them.

Still, the other 10 men were so afraid that they frightened the people listening to them. They worried about the giants. They wanted to go back to Egypt to get away from them. They cried and grumbled and had an awful time.

When God heard them, He was very angry. He said that if the people didn't want to go to the rich and beautiful land He had promised them, then He would never let them go there. Instead, they would have to live in the desert wilderness for the rest of their lives.

Only Caleb and Joshua wanted to go where God had told them to go. Those two men would get to live in the Promised Land. None of the other grown-ups ever would. But Joshua would lead the children who grew up in the wilderness. Caleb also would go with him into the land "flowing with milk and honey," the Promised Land.

I Spy

"I Spy" is a game that may be used to remind children of the purpose of the 12 people sent to explore the Promised Land. Before class, hide a variety of goods around the room that might have been found in the Promised Land: grapes, figs, other fruits and vegetables, packages of seeds, stalks of grain, a jar of honey, a small carton of milk, etc. The fruits and vegetables may be real or plastic, but if possible, have a large bunch of seedless grapes for the children to eat after all the produce has been found and brought back from the "Promised Land."

The Promised Land

Have the children sing this song with the appropriate motions. Sing it to the tune of the first part of "Oh, Dear, What Can the Matter Be?"

Come, come, come to the Promised Land. Come, come, come to the Promised Land. Come, come, come to the Promised Land	*(Beckon with both hands for the first three lines.)*
Where milk and honey are found.	*(Open arms wide.)*
We're afraid of the people there; We're afraid of the giants there; We're afraid of the cities there;	*(Jerk hands in rejecting motion, in time with music, for the first three lines.)*
They have high walls all around.	*(Join hands in closed circle above head.)*
Stay, stay, stay in the desert then. Stay, stay, stay in the desert then. Stay, stay, stay in the desert then.	*(Use bigger rejection motions.)*
Only your children shall go.	*(Put hands down to indicate short people.)*
Led by Caleb and Joshua, Led by Caleb and Joshua,	*(Hold up one finger on each hand and shake to stress.)*
Into, into the Promised Land All of your children shall go.	*(Stretch out arms in generous, inclusive gesture.)*

This song may be turned into a singing skit by having one group of children sing the first, third, and fourth stanzas, and another group sing the second.

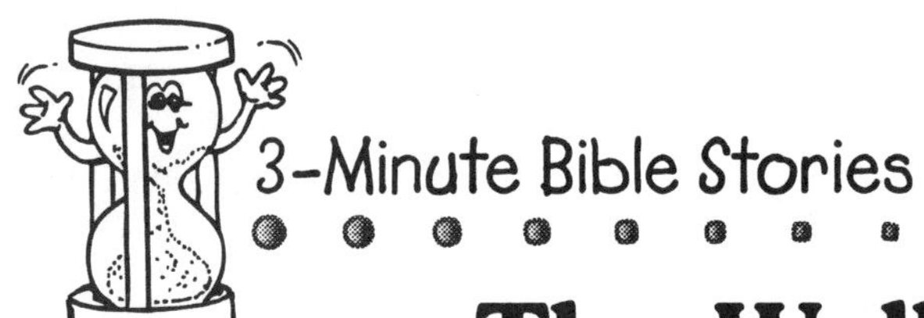

The Walls Come Down

Joshua 6:1–20

Joshua had become the leader of the Israelite people. The precious Ten Commandments had been placed in a box called the ark of the covenant. It was time for the people to go into the land that God had promised them, but obstacles stood in their way. One of these was the great walled city of Jericho.

The walls of Jericho were so thick that houses were built on top of them. The Israelites must have wondered how they would be able to take this city, but God had a plan which He told Joshua. The armed men were to march around Jericho once a day for six days. They walked in front of and behind seven priests carrying the ark of the covenant and trumpets. The priests blew the trumpets as they marched. The inhabitants of Jericho must have stood on their great walls laughing at the strange Israelites. No one could take their city this way!

On the seventh day, God told Joshua to have the priests march around the walls of Jericho seven times, blowing their trumpets. The people of Jericho must have been puzzled by these invaders. As the Israelites started around the walls for the seventh time, the priests gave one long blast on their trumpets. For the first time, all the Israelite people gave a great shout. The strong, thick walls of Jericho collapsed to the ground! Joshua and his armed men rushed across the rubble and took the city of Jericho. God had given them a great victory! The walls had come down.

Jericho Falls Down

Arrange a dozen or more large cardboard cartons in the center of the floor to represent the city of Jericho. Let one child represent a priest, carrying a horn of some kind (or with his or her hand circling his or her mouth to represent a trumpet). Let another child carry a jewel box or something comparable to represent the ark of the covenant. Have the children walk silently around the city six times, returning to their seats after each time, to mark the six days. On the seventh time, have the children keep going around seven times. When Joshua (the teacher) says, "Shout!," all the children should run forward, pushing the cartons down.

If you have a smaller space or need a less boisterous activity, this motion play may be used: *Place hands together, the palm of one on the back of the other. At the count (1st day, 2nd day, etc.), lift the top hand and bring it around the other, returning it to its original position. On the seventh day, do seven such circles; then shout and throw up your arms in rejoicing.*

Crash! Bang!

Use the hand motions described below while singing this song to the tune of "She'll Be Comin' 'Round the Mountain."

We'll go once around the city for six days. (Sh! Sh!)	*(Hold up one finger, then six fingers, then put one to the lips. Repeat for second and fifth lines.)*
We'll go once around the city for six days. (Sh! Sh!)	
We'll go once around the city.	*(Hold up one finger.)*
We'll go once around the city.	*(Hold up one finger.)*
We'll go once around the city for six days. (Sh! Sh!)	*(Repeat first line motions.)*
On the seventh, we'll go 'round it seven times. (Sh! Sh!)	*(Hold up seven fingers, then one to lips. Repeat for second line.)*
On the seventh, we'll go 'round it seven times. (Sh! Sh!)	
On the seventh, we'll go 'round it.	*(Hold up seven fingers; lower them at the end of line; then raise again.)*
On the seventh, we'll go 'round it.	
On the seventh, we'll go 'round it seven times. (Hooray!)	*(Shout and clap loudly.)*

The Very Strong Man

Judges 13:24–16:30

During the time when the Israelites were conquered by the Philistines, a special baby was born. His parents were told by an angel of God that he would free Israel. His hair was never to be cut. The baby's name was Samson, and he grew to be a very strong man.

After Samson was married, he often fought the Philistines and defeated them. They were afraid of him. To get even with Samson, the Philistines came to his wife and asked her the secret of Samson's strength, but he had not told her even though she had asked him. She was afraid but couldn't say what his secret was, so they killed her and her father.

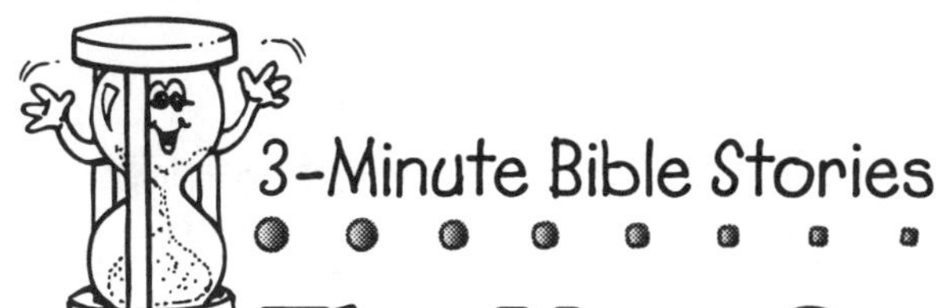

The Very Strong Man continued

In anger, Samson killed more Philistines. They went to find him to put him in prison. When they found him, Samson picked up the jawbone of a burro lying on the ground and killed 1,000 Philistine men. Then he thanked God for helping and saving him.

One day, Samson met a woman named Delilah. She was not a good person and was friendly with the Philistines. She talked Samson into telling her the secret of his strength. He told her that if his hair was cut, he would lose his strength and be like any other man.

The Philistines paid Delilah 1,000 pieces of silver to help them cut Samson's hair. When he went to sleep with his head on her lap, she called a man with a razor. The man cut off Samson's hair, and all his strength left him.

The Philistines caught Samson, as he only had ordinary strength left, and put out his eyes. They made him grind grain at the prison mill. A little later, they took him to their temple for a special celebration. They stood him among the pillars of the temple so everyone could see him and laugh at him. The temple and the pillar he was bound to were made of stone and very sturdy.

Because Samson was blind, he asked a servant who was there to help him feel the pillars supporting the temple. He said he needed to lean on them. The leaders of the Philistines were in the temple that day, along with many people, and 3,000 men and women were on the roof watching Samson.

Samson prayed and asked God to give him all his strength back so he could pull down the pillars and kill the Philistines. "Let me die with the Philistines," he prayed.

God gave him back his strength, and Samson pushed with all his might. The pillars came down and so did the temple. Samson died, but so did all those Philistines who were making life so hard for the Israelites.

Red Rover

Play this game of strength. Divide the children into teams and play a familiar game of Red Rover. Select a captain for each team. As in Red Rover, the teams join arms to make a chainlike wall. Name one team the Samson team and the other the Philistine team.

Have the Samson team shout, "Red Rover, Red Rover, send a Philistine right over." The Philistine team captain chooses a team member to run and try to break through a weak link in the Samson team. If the player breaks through, he or she may take a member of the Samson team to join his or her own team. If the player doesn't break through, he or she must join the Samson team. Then it's time for the Philistine team to shout, "Red Rover, Red Rover, send Samson right over." The captain of the Samson team chooses a team member to try to break the Philistine line.

The team that has the most members at the end of the game wins.

Indoor Olympics

Divide the children into two groups, the Israelites and the Philistines, for indoor Olympics. Keep score as each event described below is played. Encourage the teams to make up cheers to cheer on their players.

Ball Toss:
See who can throw the ball the farthest.

Plate Toss:
Have a paper plate toss to see who can come closest to a marked target.

Ping-Pong™ Hockey:
Cut out a cardboard box for a "playing field." Each player uses a straw to try to blow a Ping-Pong™ ball to the opposite goal.

Balloon Pop:
Have each child blow up a balloon, and then see who can pop the balloon first.

Lid Toss:
Draw a face on a paper plate. Cut out a big circle for the mouth. Attach the plate to a paint stick or ruler. Give each player three plastic milk bottle lids. See how many lids each one can toss through the opening of the mouth.

Dear Friend

Samson trusted in the Lord and the Lord answered his prayers.
Let the children write letters to friends about how God cares for us.

Materials: copies of the letter pattern below, crayons, glue, scissors, pencils, postage stamps

Have the children color the pattern below and then cut it out on the bold lines. Show the children how to fold on the dotted lines. Have the children write their letters on the blank sides. They can write to friends about how God cares for us. Tell them to add their return addresses on the short lines. They should write the name and address of their friends on the longer lines. Help the children seal the letters by applying glue and folding on the dotted lines. The children can apply a first-class stamp on the area shown.

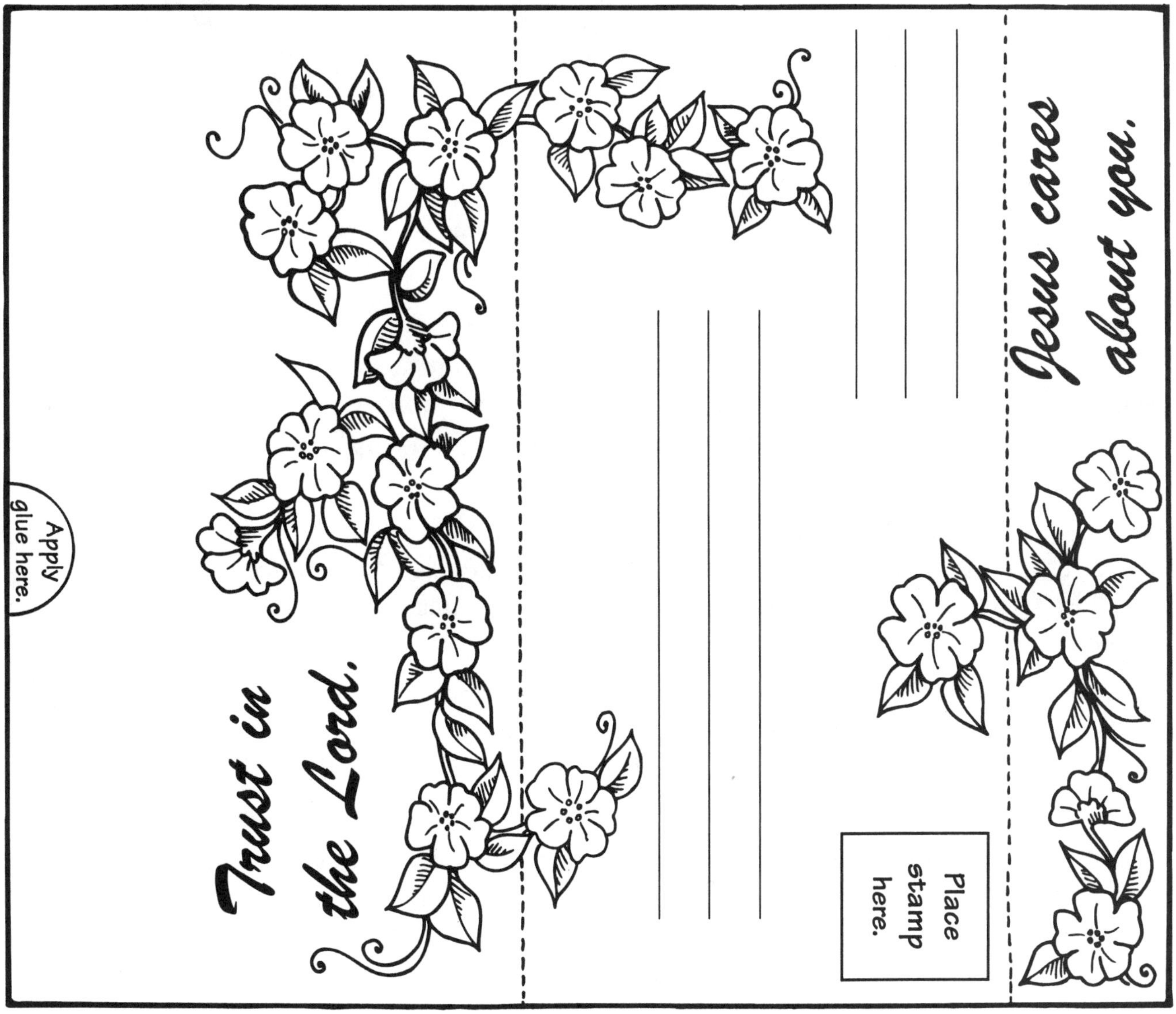

Apply glue here.

Trust in the Lord.

Place stamp here.

Jesus cares about you.

Ruth and Naomi

Ruth 1–2:12; 4:13, 17

It was a time of famine in Israel. (*Famine* means there were no crops or food.) Many people went to other countries to work and buy food. Naomi went with her husband and two sons into the land of Moab. They made a home there and stayed for many years. Naomi's two sons married Moabite girls, Orpah and Ruth.

Life was hard in Moab. Naomi's husband died; then her two sons died. The famine was no longer causing people to starve in Israel. Naomi decided that the best thing for her to do, now that she had no husband and no sons, was to go back to Israel where she had other relatives.

When she started back, Ruth and Orpah walked part of the way with her. They both loved her and were afraid they might never see her again. After they had walked some way, Naomi told her daughters-in-law that they should turn back and stay in their own land. Orpah agreed. She kissed Naomi good-bye and turned back.

But Ruth would not go back. She said she would always stay with Naomi, her mother-in-law, whom she loved. "Don't ask me to leave you," she said. *"Where you go I will go, and where you stay I will stay. Your people will be my people and your God my God. Where you die I will die, and there I will be buried . . ."* (Ruth 1:16–17) After Ruth had said this, she called on God to hear her promise that she would stay with Naomi all the rest of her life.

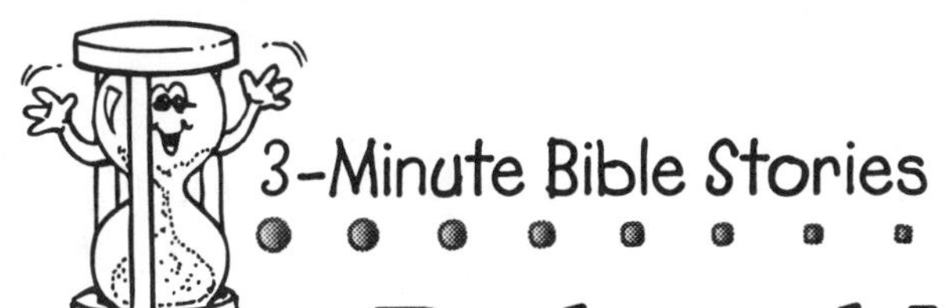

Ruth and Naomi continued

When Naomi saw that Ruth was determined, they went on together until they came to Naomi's home in Bethlehem. They lived there together, with Naomi keeping the house and Ruth going into the fields to glean. (*Glean* means that she picked up stalks of grain that the men who harvested the field had left.) By gleaning, she and Naomi had grain to make bread.

One day while Ruth was gleaning, the owner of the field came by. His name was Boaz. When he saw Ruth and heard how good she was to her mother-in-law, he decided to be good to her. He told his men to leave extra grain for her.

After a time, Boaz and Ruth were married. They had a baby whom they named Obed. Years later, Obed had a grandson named David, who became the king of Israel. King David was an ancestor of Jesus. (Ancestors are people in your family who lived before you were born.)

We remember these two women because Ruth loved Naomi so much that she went to Israel to live with her and worship God. God blessed Ruth by making her one of the ancestors of Jesus. Ruth and Boaz lived happily together and took care of Naomi as long as she lived.

The Bible verse below is a very familiar one the children can memorize. Discuss with them why Naomi was such a good person.

"Where you go I will go, and where you stay I will stay. Your people will be my people and your God my God." (Ruth 1:16b)

Heart to Heart

This activity is the perfect way to let the children know that God loves them!

Materials:
copies of the heart pattern below, construction paper, glue

Directions:
Help the children fold the sheets of construction paper into fourths like greeting cards. Using the pattern, cut out red hearts and give two to each child. Instruct the children to print "You" on one heart and "God" on the other. On the outside of the folded paper, help the children print "Good News Inside" in large letters. Have the children glue their "God" hearts on the inside left and their "You" hearts on the inside right. At the top between the two hearts, they should print the word "Loves." Suggest that they give the cards to people who do not attend church or to those who need cheering up.

Ruth's Promise

Let one child be Ruth while all the rest act as a chorus, saying the introductory words of her promise. This may be done several times with different girls taking the part of Ruth.

Chorus	Ruth
Don't urge me to leave you	Or to turn back from you.
Where you go,	I will go,
And where you stay,	I will stay.
Your people will be my people	And your God my God.
Where you die	I will die, and there I will be buried!

Teacher: And that's the promise that Ruth kept all her life.

A Gleaning Game

Scatter several dozen paper or plastic straws on the floor to represent grain left by reapers. Then choose a child to be Naomi, sitting on the floor at one side of the room where she is at home. Everybody else gleans, picking up as many straws as possible with one hand. When all the straws have been picked up, each child brings his or her handful to Naomi. Help Naomi count each child's straws. The one who has the most is named Ruth. Naomi may then reward each one with a cracker, such as might have been made from the grain.

A Call From God

1 Samuel 3

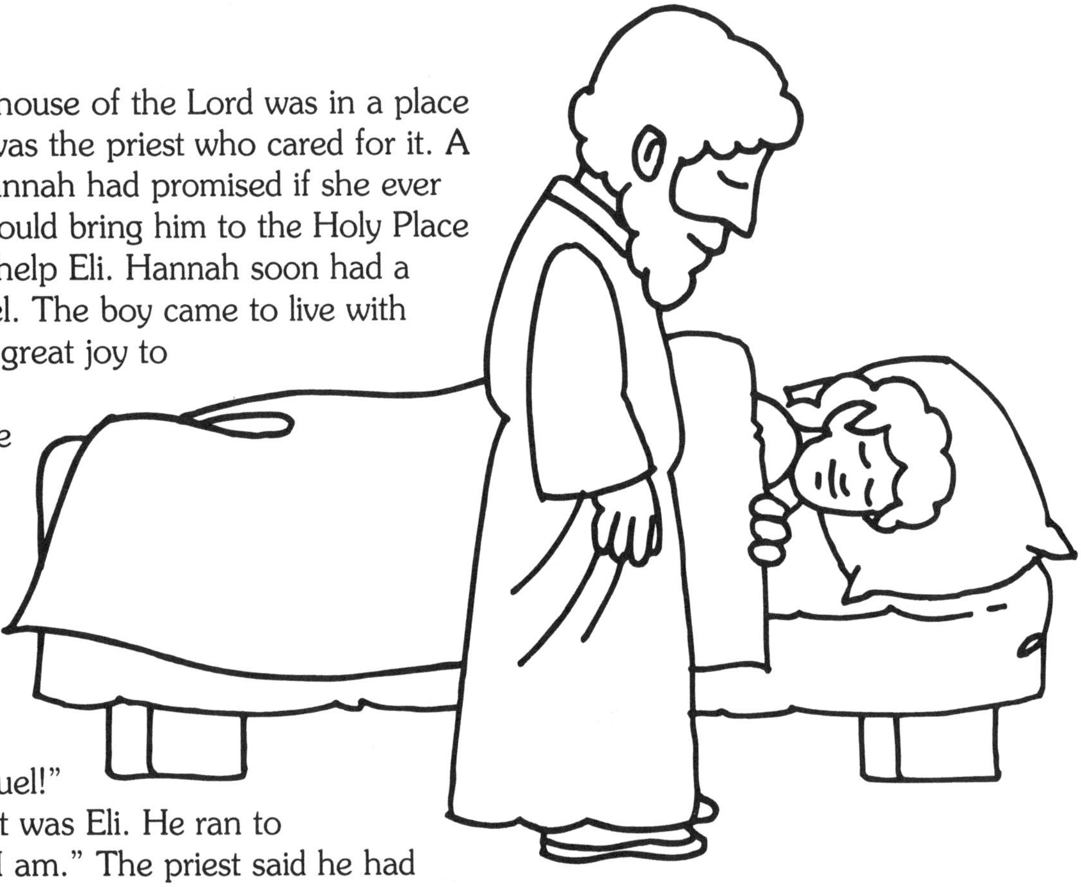

Long ago, the house of the Lord was in a place called Shiloh. Eli was the priest who cared for it. A woman named Hannah had promised if she ever had a child, she would bring him to the Holy Place to serve God and help Eli. Hannah soon had a son named Samuel. The boy came to live with Eli. Samuel was a great joy to the elderly priest. His own sons were wicked and made Eli very sad.

One night when Eli and Samuel were asleep, Samuel heard a voice calling him. "Samuel!" The boy thought it was Eli. He ran to Eli saying, "Here I am." The priest said he had not called Samuel and told him to lie back down. Samuel obeyed.

Shortly, Samuel heard the voice again saying, "Samuel!" For the second time, Samuel rushed to Eli. Again the priest said he had not called him.

For a third time, the boy heard someone call, "Samuel!" He ran again to Eli. The priest realized that this must be God calling Samuel. He told the boy, "Go and lie down. If the voice calls again, speak to Him, for it is the Lord."

As Samuel lay there, God called, "Samuel! Samuel!" Samuel said, "Speak, for your servant is listening."

The Lord told Samuel that Eli's wicked sons were going to be punished. The next morning, the priest insisted that Samuel tell him what God had said. Samuel told Eli everything. From that time on, people all over Israel knew that Samuel was a messenger for God.

The Bible verse below is an easy one for the children to remember when they say it while playing with the "phones" they make in "Telephone Fun" below.

Then Samuel said, "Speak, for your servant is listening." (1 Samuel 3:10b)

Telephone Fun

These phones make acting out the story of God calling to Samuel a lot of fun.

Materials:

Styrofoam™ cups or tin cans
string
a small screwdriver
scissors
yardstick
paper clips

Directions:

Punch a hole in the bottom of each cup or can with the screwdriver. Help children insert the ends of a six-foot length of string into the cups or cans. Tie each end to a paper clip so that the string stays in the cups. Have pairs of children speak through their "phones." They can also act out the story of God calling to Samuel. You might also suggest conversations you would like the children to have, for example, call someone who is sick, call a person you have hurt to apologize, ask a friend to come to church, call a Bible character (Jonah, Ruth, Moses, Peter, Daniel, etc.) and talk about his or her adventures. Suggest that the children go home and call someone who would enjoy hearing from them: a shut-in, older relative, sick person, lonely neighbor, etc.

Fun With Samuel

This craft is a nice way for the children to remember this Bible story.

Materials:
copies of the patterns on this page, crayons, scissors, brad fasteners

Directions:

1. Have the children color pieces A and B and cut them out on the bold lines.
2. Help the children insert a brad fastener through the figure of Samuel where the black dot is and then through the black dot in the picture.
3. The children can move the boy's body to sit up or lie down.

A

B

"Here I am, Lord.
I will obey You."

Here I Am

This choral speaking may be done several times with different members of the group taking the solo part.

Solo:	Here I am. Here I am.	*(Raise arms toward heaven.)* *(Bring arms back to chest.)*
Chorus:	That was Samuel's answer.	
Solo:	Here I am.	*(Raise arms, then bring them back to chest.)*
Chorus:	Here we are.	*(All raise arms toward heaven.)*
Solo:	That shall be our answer, Lord, Whenever You shall call.	*(Raise arms again.)*
Chorus:	Here we are, Lord! Here we are!	*(All raise arms toward heaven and hold them up.)*

The Calling of Samuel

Hold up a small stone (or toy or ball small enough to be concealed in a child's hand). One child is designated as Samuel and leaves the room. The other children form a circle, sitting on the floor and holding out their hands. You go all around the circle, touching each pair of hands, leaving the stone in one. Each child closes his or her hands as you pass so no one else knows who has the stone.

You then call, "Samuel." The missing child comes back in. He or she looks at the children's closed hands and faces. They pretend guilt or innocence to keep "Samuel" from knowing who has the stone. "Samuel" has three guesses. If one is right, the person holding the stone becomes Samuel for the continuing game. If none of Samuel's guesses is right, he or she must go out and try again (or "Samuel" may be allowed to choose someone to be the next Samuel).

David and the Sling

1 Samuel 16–17

Samuel was sent by God to find a new king for the people of Israel. Saul had been chosen, but he had displeased God. Samuel journeyed to Bethlehem to the home of Jesse, who had many sons.

Seven of Jesse's sons were all rejected by God. Samuel asked Jesse if he had any other sons. Jesse replied that the youngest, David, was out tending the sheep. Samuel sent for David. When he entered, the Lord told Samuel, *"Rise and anoint him; he is the one."* (1 Samuel 16:12) Israel had a new king! But David was very young and not ready to become a king. He had much to learn, and Saul was still in charge.

Saul was tormented by evil spirits. He asked his attendants to find someone who could play a harp. The person they brought was David, who often sang and played as he watched the sheep. David's harp music soothed the troubled ruler.

Soon after that, Saul's army was at war with the Philistines. The enemy had a champion named Goliath who was over nine feet tall! No one in Saul's army dared fight him. Three of Jesse's sons were in the army, so David's father sent him to check on them.

After a long walk, David got to where his brothers were with Saul's army. "Father sent you some food," he told his brothers. "He says you'll be needing it."

The brothers eagerly tore open the package. "That's wonderful," they said. "We were hungry!"

At that moment, an extremely frightening warrior, a giant of a man, came forward from the Philistine army. He was wearing heavy bronze armor and a helmet. He shouted, *"Choose a man and have him come down to me. If he is able to fight and kill me, we will become your subjects; but if I overcome him and kill him, you will become our subjects and serve us."* (1 Samuel 17:8–9)

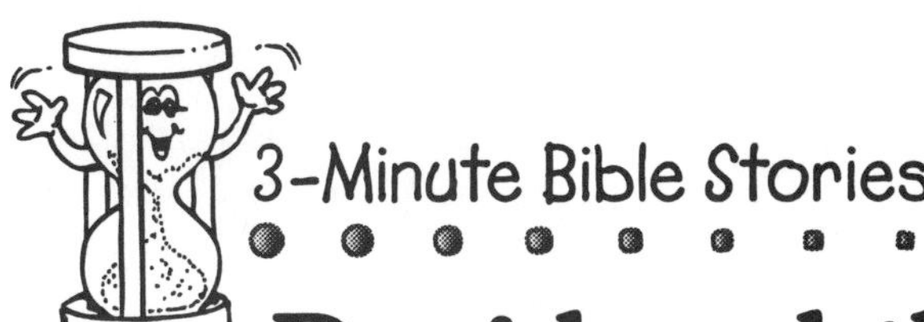

David and the Sling continued

David swung his sling, thinking. He went to see King Saul. David said to him, "I want to fight this giant Philistine. God will protect me."

Saul said to David, "Go and may the Lord be with you."

David picked up five smooth, round rocks. He put one into the pouch of his sling. He prayed as he walked toward the giant. Goliath roared with laughter. *"Am I a dog, that you come at me with sticks?"* (1 Samuel 17:43) he asked. He raised his great spear, with the shining sharp point, and walked toward David.

David continued walking forward, too, swinging his sling at his side. *"I come against you in the name of the Lord Almighty, the God of the armies of Israel,"* (1 Samuel 17:45) he said.

As David got closer, he swung the sling around and around, faster and faster. Goliath ran toward him, his terrible spear still raised and ready to throw. David let the stone fly.

Whump! It wasn't a very loud noise, but Goliath stopped. His body fell to the earth. Clang! His armor hit the ground. The small rock had hit him right between the eyes.

David walked quietly forward and looked down at the giant. Then he quietly prayed and thanked God for helping him defeat the giant.

When the Israelite army saw that the giant was dead, they began to chase the Philistine army. With God's help, David, a shepherd boy, had won the battle!

David Did It!

This is a fun way to remind the children what David did. They can also use the activity for other Bible characters.

Materials:
copies of the patterns below, paper, glue, crayons

Directions:
Give each child a set of patterns to color and cut out. Next, they glue the patterns to a sheet of paper. Then the children can write or dictate several sentences telling about David and the pictures. (Examples: He killed a giant. He was anointed by Samuel. He sang and wrote psalms. He cared for his father's sheep.) Have the children write "David" at the top of their papers.

crook

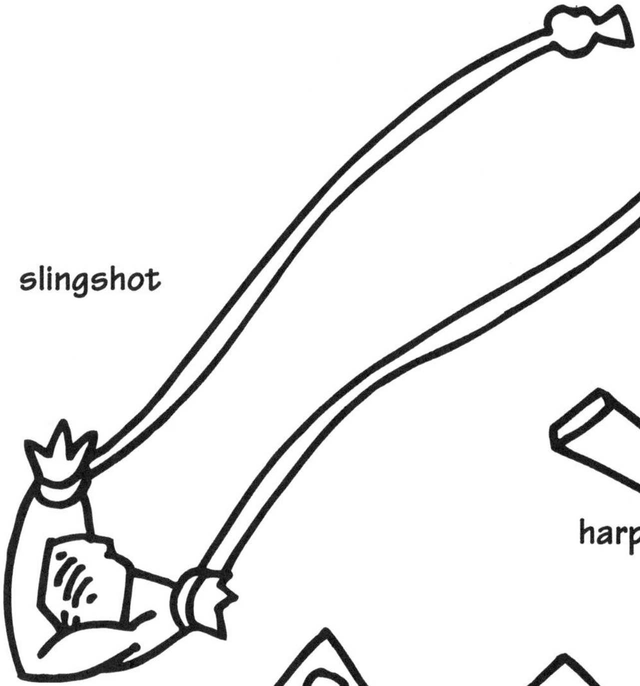

slingshot

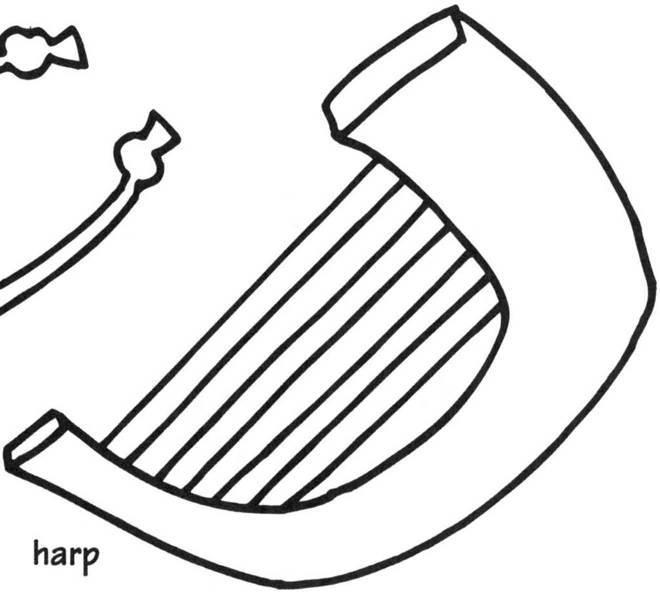

harp

crown

I Am Not Afraid

This door hanger is fun for the children to make and will remind them that God will protect them.

Materials:
copies of the door hanger pattern below, lightweight cardboard or posterboard, crayons, cotton balls, scissors, glue

Have each child color the door hanger below and glue it to lightweight cardboard or posterboard. Next, they cut it out on the bold lines. Then the children can fold it on the dotted lines and cut out where indicated. Finally, tell the children to use glue to fasten both sides together and to attach a cotton ball to the sheep.

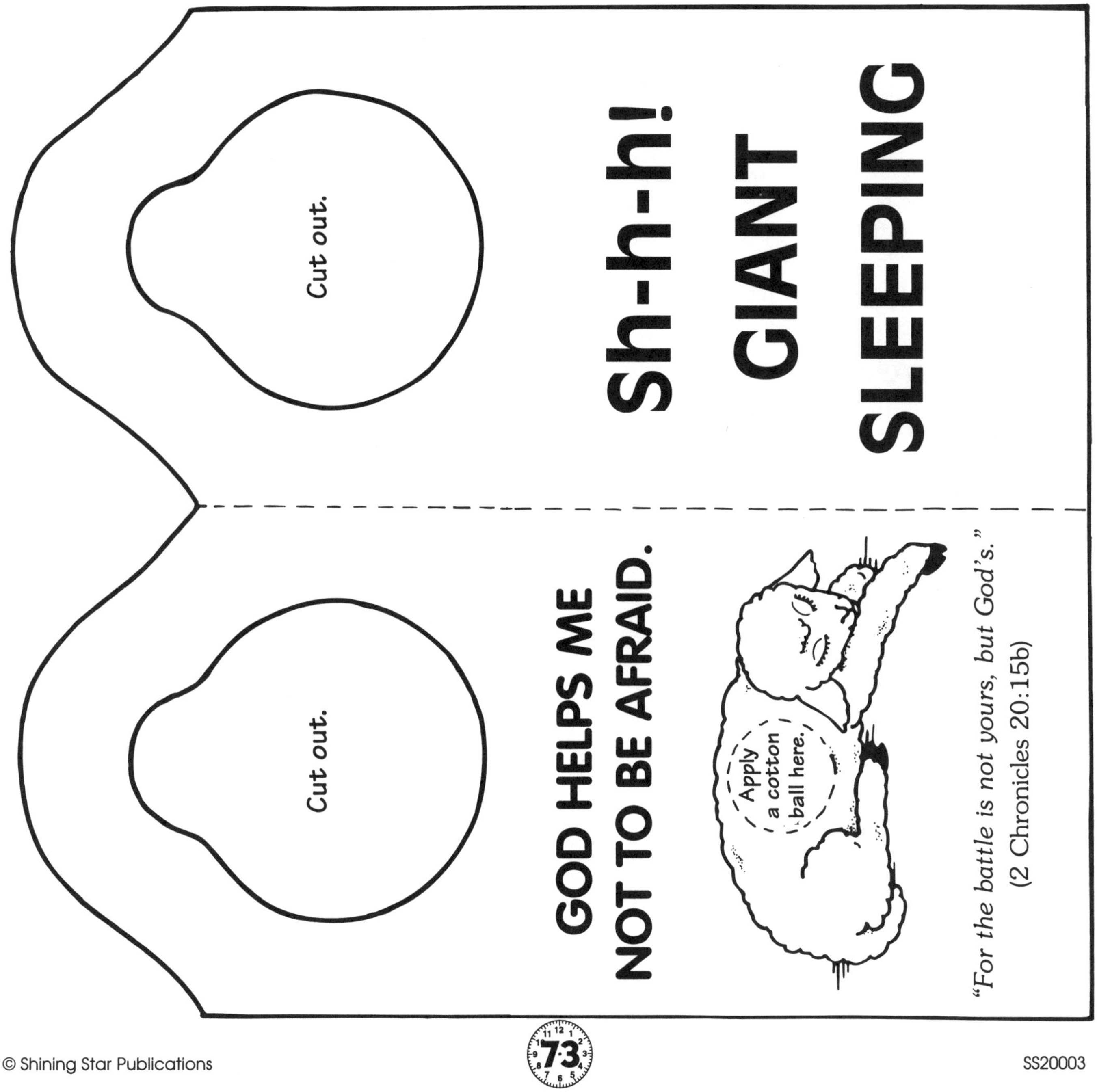

Cut out.

Sh-h-h!
GIANT
SLEEPING

Cut out.

GOD HELPS ME
NOT TO BE AFRAID.

Apply a cotton ball here.

"For the battle is not yours, but God's."
(2 Chronicles 20:15b)

Cardboard Armor

David did not want to wear armor, but chances are the children in your care would want to if they had to fight a giant! Help them make their own cardboard armor.

Materials:

three cardboard fruit box dividers per child
yarn
felt strips
newspapers
stapler
tape
hole punch
large nail

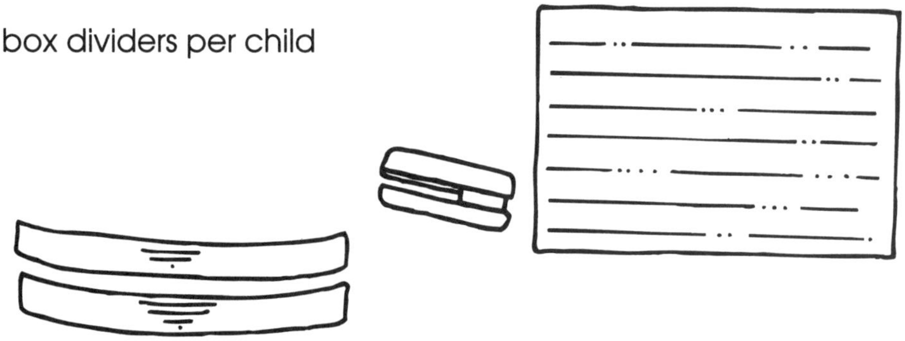

Directions:

Ask a produce worker at your local market for cardboard fruit box dividers (apple season is a good time to find them). Punch a hole about halfway down each side of two of the dividers and tie a 12" piece of yarn through each hole. Cut two 1" x 9" strips of felt and staple them to the top of these dividers, joining the two pieces. Be careful that the felt is far enough apart for the "armor" to fit over the child's head. Once the armor is in place, secure by tying the pieces of yarn.

Armor

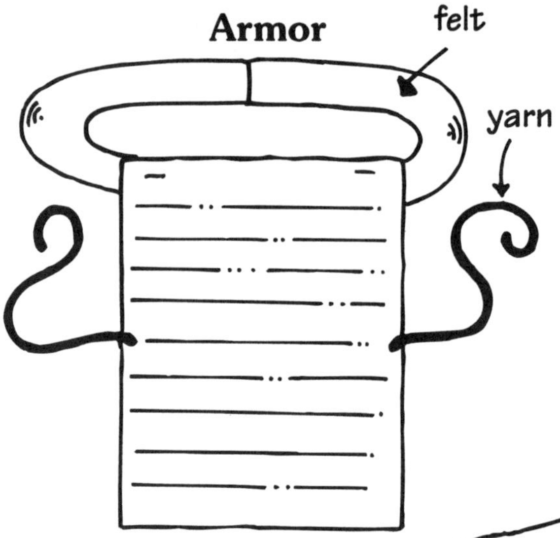

felt

yarn

Shield

Use a fruit box divider to make a shield. Using the nail, punch two holes in the center and tie a piece of yarn through so the child can hold onto the "shield" from the back.

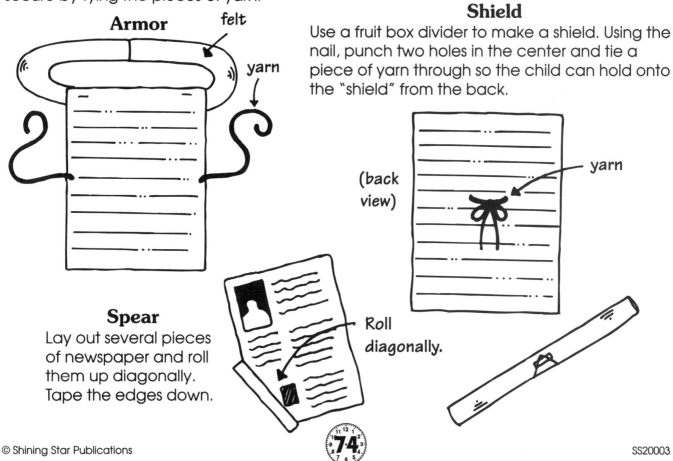

(back view)

yarn

Spear

Lay out several pieces of newspaper and roll them up diagonally. Tape the edges down.

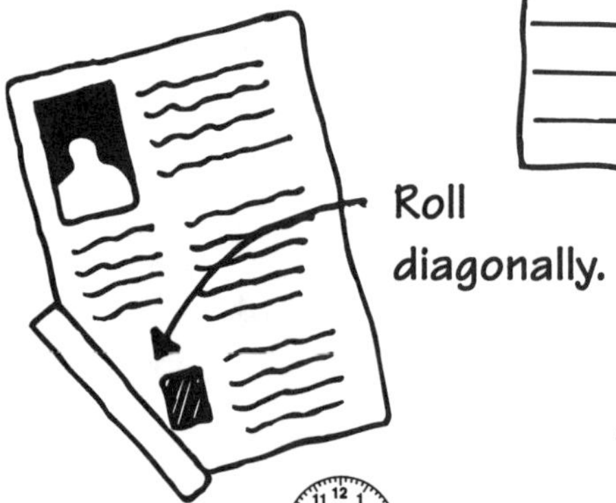

Roll diagonally.

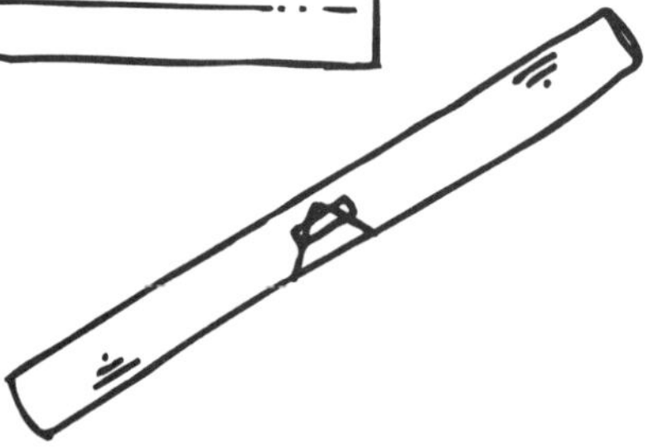

David's Harp

Let the children create their own "harps" to use to play beautiful music to the Lord.

Materials:
heavy cardboard
three colored rubber bands per child
six brad fasteners per child
copies of the harp pattern below
scissors

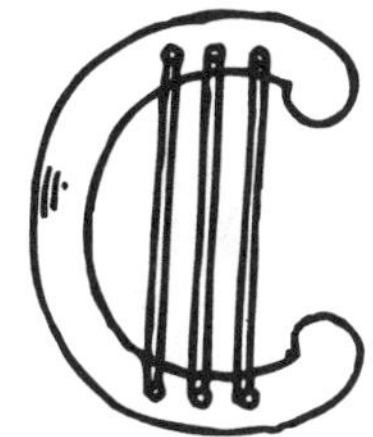

Directions:
Help the children trace the harp pattern below on a heavy piece of cardboard and cut it out. Show them how to put the brad fasteners where the Xs are. Next, they hook a rubber band around the brad at the top. Then they secure the back end of the brad and hold the rubber band in place while hooking the rubber band on the parallel brad. Tell them to do this with all three rubber bands.

When the harp is completed, the children can sing the words below to the tune of "You Are My Sunshine" and strum along.

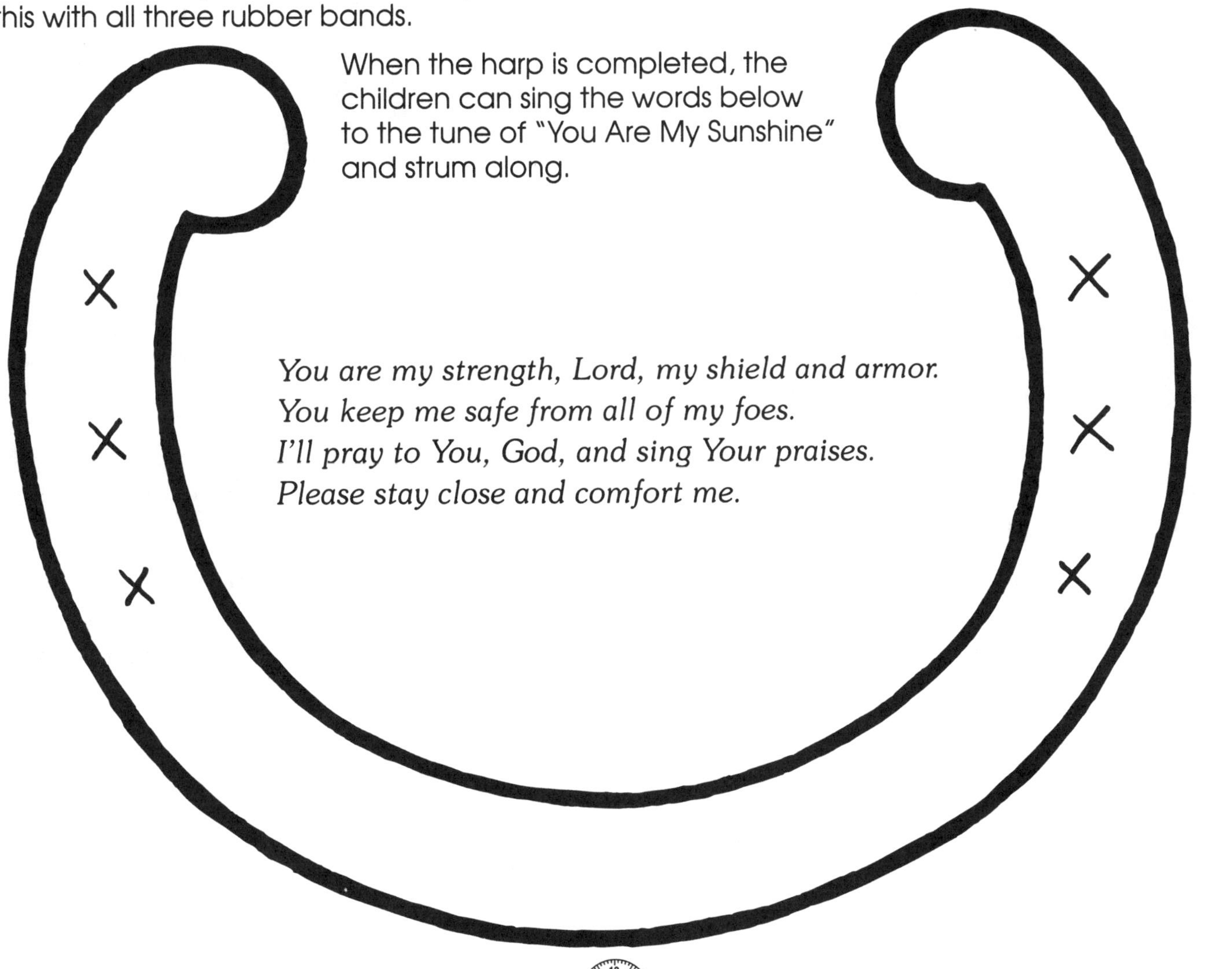

X X
X X
X X

You are my strength, Lord, my shield and armor.
You keep me safe from all of my foes.
I'll pray to You, God, and sing Your praises.
Please stay close and comfort me.

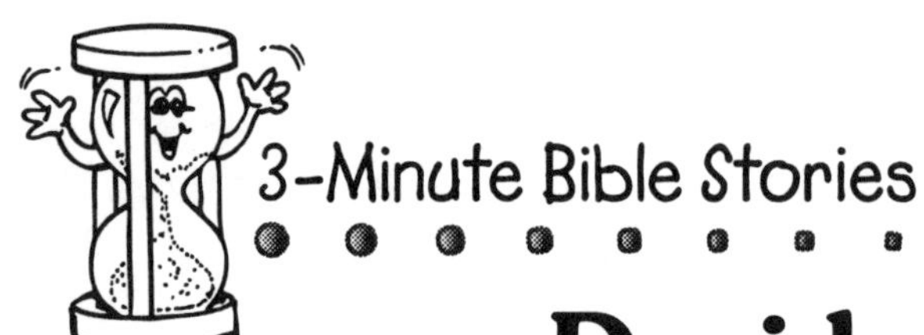

David and Jonathan

1 Samuel 18:1–9; 20:1–42

After David killed the giant Goliath, the Israelites were grateful and very proud of him. King Saul honored him even though David was only a shepherd boy. Saul gave him a place in his own household. He made him an officer in the army. Often, Saul had David play on the harp because the king liked to listen to music.

Saul's son, Jonathan, and David became very good friends. Jonathan gave David his own beautiful robe, a sword, and a bow with arrows. David and Jonathan made a covenant (a promise or agreement) that they would be best friends forever.

At first, everything went well. David did whatever King Saul asked of him. In fact, the trouble began because David did everything so well. He became so popular that a song was written about him. When he came back from battle, women danced in the streets and sang, "Saul has slain his thousands, and David his tens of thousands."

That made King Saul jealous. It sounded as if David was a greater fighter than the king! From then on, Saul hated him and made up his mind to kill David.

David realized that the king was his enemy, but Jonathan didn't think so. He could not believe that his own father would be an enemy of his best friend. Jonathan made a plan to find out for sure how his father felt about David.

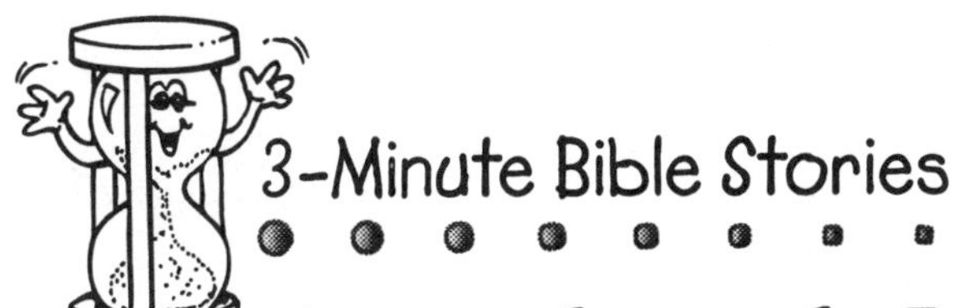

David and Jonathan continued

According to the plan, David would not come to supper for two nights. Instead, he would hide by a big rock in a field. During that time, Jonathan would talk with his father. He would find out how Saul felt about David. Then Jonathan would go to the field where David was hiding and shoot arrows near the rock. He would bring a servant with him to collect the arrows.

This was the secret code Jonathan planned. He might shout to his servant, "The arrows are on this side of you. Bring them here." That would mean that David could come to him. Saul was not angry. But if Jonathan shouted, "The arrows are beyond you," David must go away from him to be safe.

Jonathan talked with his father and found out that Saul was very jealous of David. He even said that David must die! Jonathan was so upset that he couldn't even eat his supper.

In the morning, Jonathan went to the field and shot arrows. He shouted to his servant, "Isn't the arrow beyond you? Hurry! Go quickly." This was Jonathan's way of warning David of what danger he was in.

Jonathan sent the servant home with his bow and arrows. After the servant had gone, Jonathan ran to the place where David was hiding. David and Jonathan said good-bye.

Before David left, Jonathan reminded him of their covenant. No matter how Saul felt, they had promised to be friends forever. This is why, when we speak of good friends today, we remember David and Jonathan.

They Were Friends

Sing this song to the tune of "The Bear Came Over the Mountain."

David and Jonathan, they were friends.
David and Jonathan, they were friends.
David and Jonathan, they were friends
A long, long time ago.

Jonathan's father was David's foe.
Jonathan's father was David's foe.
Jonathan's father was David's foe
A long, long time ago.

David was hiding away from Saul.
David was hiding away from Saul.
David was hiding away from Saul
When Jonathan drew his bow.

He shot an arrow beyond the rock.
He shot an arrow beyond the rock.
He shot an arrow beyond the rock
To tell his friend to go.

David and Jonathan, they were friends.
David and Jonathan, they were friends.
David and Jonathan, they were friends
Wherever they might go.

David and Jonathan

Divide the children into pairs. Each pair forms a David-and-Jonathan team, one standing behind the other, holding him or her by the shoulders. One or two single players left are "Saul"(s). "Saul" tries to attach himself or herself to a team by putting his or her hands on the shoulders of any second team member. The pairs twist and turn to try to keep him or her from doing so. When "Saul" does succeed, the front one of the pair must drop off and become Saul. "Saul" then tries to attach himself or herself to some other pair. The game continues as different Davids have to drop and become Saul.

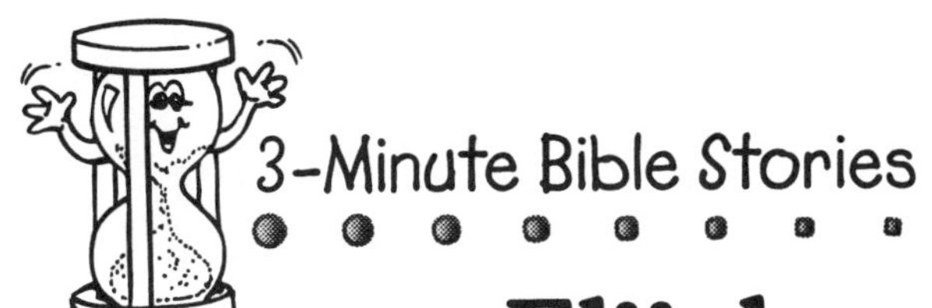

Elijah and the Ravens

1 Kings 16:30–33; 17:1–6

Elijah was a great prophet of the Lord who did many wonderful things. One of the things he is most remembered for is not what he did, but what God did for him. God protected him when wicked King Ahab wanted to kill him.

Ahab was king of Israel. He did more bad things than any of the kings before him. He married an evil woman named Jezebel who had many of the Lord's prophets killed. Ahab made an idol to Jezebel's false god, Baal, and worshipped the idol instead of the Lord.

Elijah scolded Ahab for his sins and tried to get Ahab to change his wicked ways. Ahab would not listen. He just got worse and worse.

Finally, Elijah warned Ahab of punishment to come. There was going to be a terrible drought in Israel. Elijah said, "There will be neither dew nor rain in the next few years unless I call for it in the name of the Lord, the God of Israel." That meant there would be no water for anybody in the country as long as Ahab continued his wickedness.

The Lord knew Ahab would be angry with Elijah. Ahab would probably try to kill him. So God told Elijah to leave the place where he was, where Ahab's men could find him, and go east to hide in the Kerith Valley, east of the Jordan River. That would be outside Ahab's kingdom. Elijah could drink from Kerith Brook. He would have water while all the rivers in Ahab's kingdom were drying up.

Elijah . . . continued

Elijah did as the Lord told him and escaped from Ahab. He still did not know how he was to get food. He had to stay hidden in the Kerith Valley, but he trusted God to take care of him.

God knew Elijah's needs, and He was so great He could command everything in nature. He told the ravens that lived near Kerith Brook to help Elijah. (Ravens are big black birds, bigger than crows.) They were to bring bread and meat every morning to the bank of the Kerith Brook where Elijah would be waiting for them. In the evening, they were to bring more bread and meat to the same place.

For many days, Elijah drank water from the Kerith Brook and ate food that the Lord sent to him by the ravens. He was safe from Ahab in Kerith Valley, and he had water and food, while Ahab's country was drying up. God took good care of Elijah.

Feeding Elijah Relay Race

Choose a child to be Elijah. Then divide the rest of the children into two groups, one to carry meat and one to carry bread to Elijah. Give each child in one group a representation of bread (a card with the word on it or a picture of bread). Give each child in the other group a similar representation of meat. Have Elijah sit in the front of the room and have the two teams line up at the back. Give each leader a small basket.

At the starting signal, the leader in each row puts his or her bread or meat into the basket and "flies" to Elijah, holding the basket with arms waving. He or she empties the basket by Elijah and flies back to give the next person in line the basket. Whichever line gets all its bread or meat to Elijah first wins.

Go, Elijah, Go

Sing this song to the tune of "Old MacDonald Had a Farm."

Old Elijah ran away—Go, Elijah, go—
When unto him the Lord did say, "Go, Elijah, go.
Find the Kerith Valley
With its cool, cool brook,
Where Ahab will not think to look.
There I'll keep you safe indeed.
Elijah, you'll have all you need."

Old Elijah ran away—Go, Elijah, go—
When unto him the Lord did say, "Go, Elijah, go."
He found Kerith Brook
With its water sweet,
And ravens brought him bread and meat
He had good water, and he was fed.
Elijah did what God had said.

God Provides for Us

God provided Elijah with the food and water he needed. God also provides the children with the things they need. The craft below will help remind them of this.

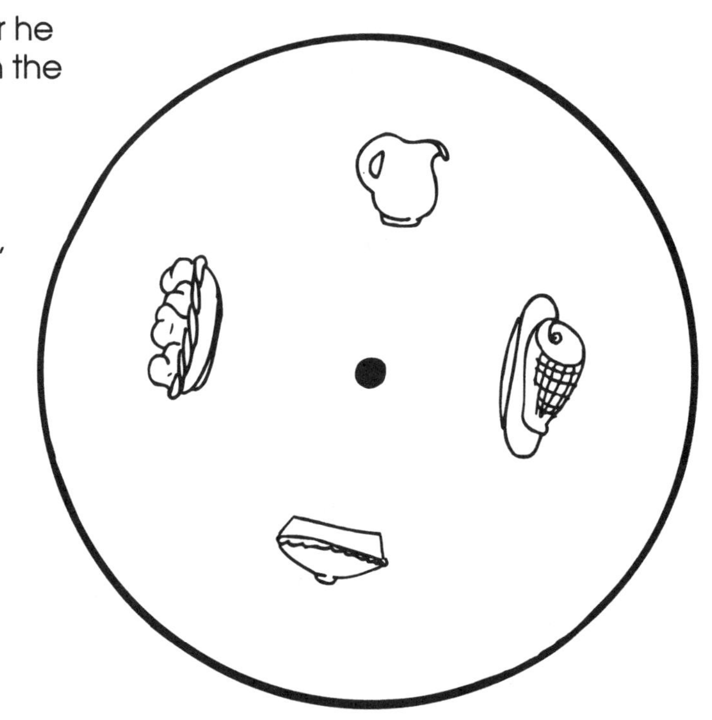

Materials:
copies of the patterns on this page, crayons, scissors, brad fasteners

Directions:

1. Have the children color the two patterns and cut them out on the bold lines.
2. Help them insert a brad fastener through the black dot in the picture and then through the center of the wheel.
3. The children can turn their wheel to see the food on the table.

God Provides
Cut out.
for Our Needs.

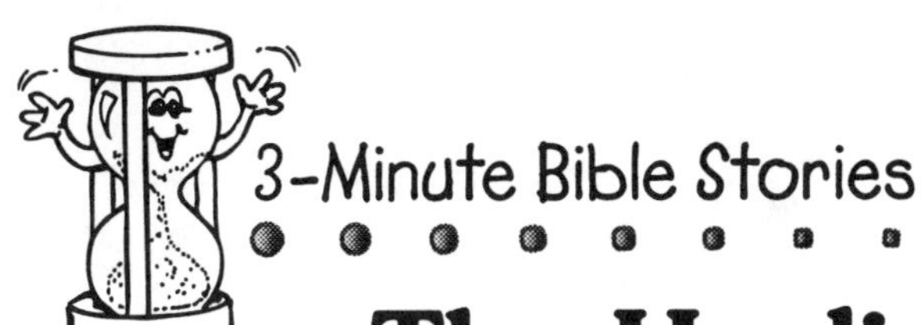

The Healing Power of God

1 Kings 17:17–24

A widow and her son gave Elijah a place to live in their home. God provided food for all three of them while there was a drought in the land.

One day, the widow's son became sick and died. The widow said to Elijah, "What do you have against me, man of God? Did you come to remind me of my sin and kill my son?"

"Give me your son," Elijah said. He carried the boy to his upstairs bedroom. He laid the boy on his bed. Then he cried out to the Lord, "Oh Lord my God, have you brought tragedy upon this widow I am staying with by letting her son die?"

Elijah stretched himself out over the boy three times and cried out again, "Oh Lord my God, let this boy's life return to him!" God heard Elijah's prayer and the boy revived.

Elijah carried him downstairs.

"Look," he told the boy's mother, "your son is alive!"

The woman said to Elijah, "Now I know that you are a man of God and that the Word of the Lord from your mouth is the truth."

SS20003

God Cares!

The children can color, cut out, and hang this poster at home to remind them that God cares!

Materials:
copies of the poster below, markers or crayons, scissors, gold and silver glitter, glue

Directions:

1. Have the children color and cut out the poster below.
2. Show them how to decorate it with gold and silver glitter.

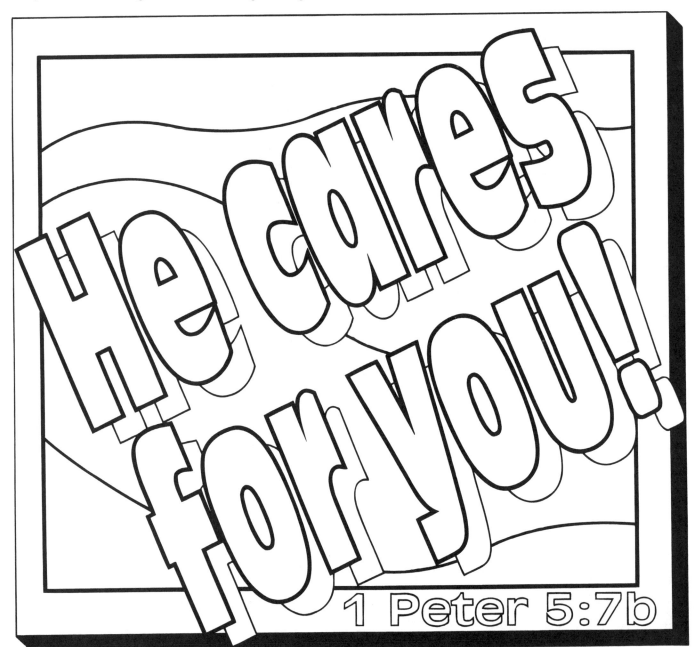

He cares for you!!

1 Peter 5:7b

Queen Esther

Esther 2:5–4:16; 8:3–11

Esther was a beautiful Jewish girl who lived in Persia long, long ago. After her mother and father died, she was adopted and brought up by her cousin, Mordecai. Esther was a kind girl, and everybody liked her.

The king of Persia was looking for a new queen. Many pretty girls were brought for him to choose from. When he saw Esther, he chose her and set the royal crown on her head. She became Queen Esther.

There was much celebration in the country of Persia. The king had a great banquet and gave gifts to many people. He did not know or care that Esther was Jewish. She was beautiful and kind, and he admired her.

Some time after Esther became queen, two men plotted to kill the king. Esther's cousin, Mordecai, found out about the plot and sent word to her. She told the king, and his life was saved. He was very grateful to Mordecai.

One man in the king's court, named Haman, was very jealous of Esther's cousin. Haman, the king's adviser, knew that Mordecai was Jewish, so he planned to have all the Jewish people in the whole kingdom killed. Haman thought he would get rid of Mordecai that way. When Mordecai heard of this terrible plan, he sent word to Esther. He asked her to talk to the king to save her people.

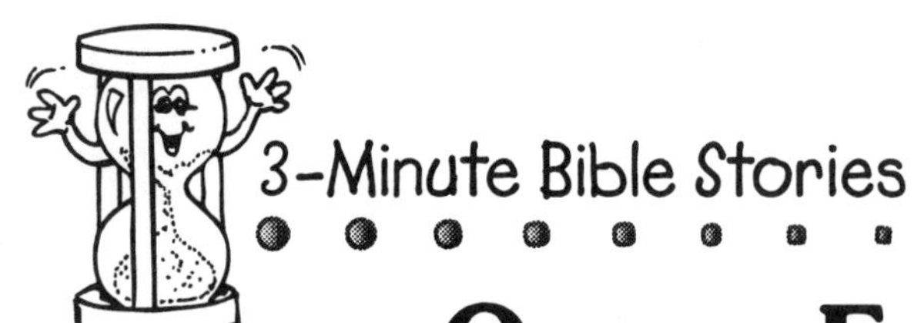

Queen Esther continued

Queen Esther didn't know what to do. She was not supposed to go before the king unless he called for her. He could even order her to be killed if she disobeyed that rule. She sent word to Mordecai about how dangerous it would be for her to try to talk to the king.

Mordecai sent a stern message back to her: "You must save your people. Who knows? Maybe God made you queen for this very reason, to save your people."

Esther was worried. She wanted to save her family and friends, but what if the king ordered her to be killed? She made up her mind that whatever happened, she must talk to the king. She must ask him not to do this terrible thing that Haman had planned.

Queen Esther sent her answer to Mordecai. She told him to have all the Jewish people get together and fast for three days (that meant that they would not eat or drink for three days) while they prayed to God to take care of her and her people. She and all the maids in her palace would fast and pray, too. Then she would go to the king.

Queen Esther finished her message with brave words, "If I die, I die." She meant that she would do the best she could. If she was killed, at least she would have tried to save her people.

Queen Esther did not die. She was able to convince the king. He issued an order that gave the Jewish people the right to defend themselves. From that day to this, Queen Esther has been honored for risking her life to save her people.

Queen Esther's Crown

Make a tagboard or construction paper crown with gold cord and sequin decorations on the front. Then on the floor, mark two circles in chalk at a distance from each other.

Players take turns standing in a circle and trying to throw the crown into the other circle. If it touches the circle, a player gets two points. If it lands inside the circle, a player gets five points. The tossing may be repeated until one person has a score of 10 or 20, or until time runs out. The highest scorer gets to wear the crown home.

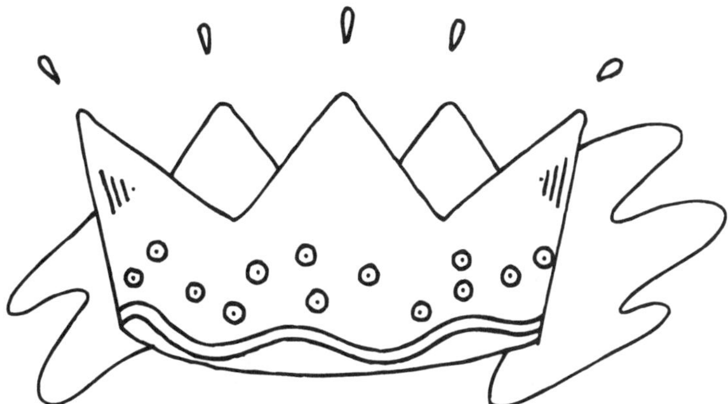

Saved by Queen Esther

Sing this song with appropriate motions to the tune of "Good King Wenceslas."

Haman planned to kill all Jews In every Persian city.	*(Spread both hands out, palms and thumbs down.)*
No one else dared tell the king	*(Shake head.)*
Or ask him to take pity.	*(Clasp hands and bow.)*
Good Queen Esther, she was brave;	*(Put hand on heart.)*
Her people she did cherish.	*(Do hugging motion.)*
She would ask the king herself,	*(Lift right hand as if taking an oath.)*
Even if she perished.	*(Shrug.)*
To the great hall Esther went,	*(Clasp hands and bow.)*
And asked the king to save them.	
He loved Esther and agreed;	*(Nod head.)*
The right to live he gave them.	*(Extend hands, palms up.)*
Good Queen Esther, she was brave;	*(Put hand on heart.)*
Her people she did cherish.	*(Do hugging motion.)*
Because she dared to do God's will	*(Lift right hand.)*
He did not let her perish!	*(Smile and shake head.)*

Faithful Daniel

Daniel 6

Daniel was a boy when he was captured and taken to Babylon, but he was faithful to God. He declared he would not eat any food that had been offered to an idol. Daniel grew strong and wise and became a powerful man in Babylon.

Darius was king. He liked Daniel, but others were jealous and wanted to kill him. They asked Darius to make a decree that for 30 days, no one could pray to any other god but the king. If they disobeyed, they would be killed by lions. (The men knew that Daniel prayed three times a day to his God.) Vain Darius agreed.

Daniel knew about the decree and knew if he prayed, he could die. This did not stop faithful Daniel. He prayed as he always had, and the evil men rushed to tell King Darius. The sad king had to put Daniel in the lions' den. As he turned away, Darius said he hoped Daniel's God would rescue him. King Darius did not sleep well that night.

As Daniel stood among the lions, he was not afraid, for he knew he had been true to God. Suddenly, an angel appeared and shut the lions' mouths so they could not harm Daniel. The angel went away, and Daniel slept peacefully among the lions.

The next morning at dawn, King Darius returned. He called to Daniel, asking if his God had saved him. The king was overjoyed when he heard Daniel's voice come up from the den saying he had been saved by an angel. Daniel was taken from the lions' den, and the men who had accused him were put in it. Daniel was safe because he had trusted God and remained faithful to Him.

Finger Puppet Fun

These are fun for the children to make to retell the story of "Daniel in the Lions' Den."

Materials:
copies of the patterns below, paper, tape or glue

Directions:
Give each child a copy of the patterns. Have the children color, cut out, and tape or glue the ends together to fit their fingers. Then let them act out the story of "Faithful Daniel". Have them memorize and include this Bible verse in their stories:

"My God sent his angel, and he shut the mouths of the lions. They have not hurt me, because I was found innocent in his sight." (Daniel 6:22a)

Daniel

Darius

angel

lion

Musical Instruments

Let the children have fun making the musical instruments described below for a marching parade to celebrate Daniel's escape.

Drum:
Spray paint an empty oatmeal carton and let it dry. Punch a hole on each side, 2"–3" below the top. Thread enough string through the hole so it can be hung around the child's neck as he or she marches along and beats on the drum.

Pie Pan Jangle:
Punch 4–6 holes around the edge of a disposable pie pan. Thread yarn or string through the holes and attach small bells. Have children shake their instruments as they march along.

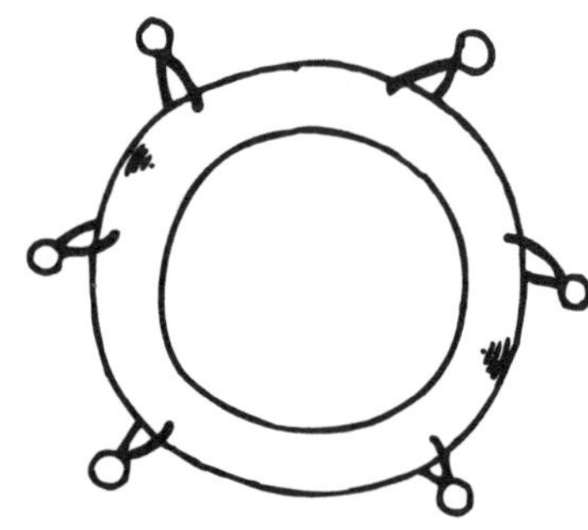

Shaker:
Fill an empty coffee can one-fourth full with small pebbles or beans. Cover it with a plastic lid. A child may shake it back and forth as he or she marches along.

Parade Flags:
Design flags using old pillowcases. With markers or paints, draw pictures or designs on the cases to represent God's army marching along. Sew a piece of yarn to the top and bottom of each pillowcase and tie it to a stick. Let children wave the flags as they march along.

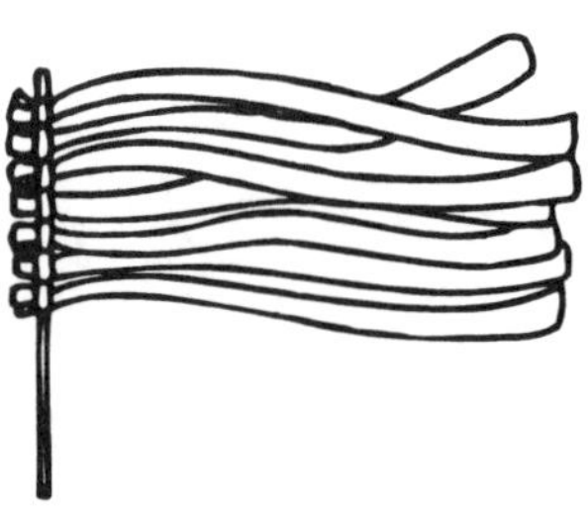

Parade Streamers:
Tie several long, thin pieces of colorful crepe paper to a stick. Show children how to make circle eights with the streamers in the air as they march along.

Sounds for the Story of Daniel

Ask the children to make the following sounds and motions as the story on page 88 is read:

1. Every time the lions' den is mentioned, growl (grrr) and hold up both hands with fingers curved like claws.
2. When Daniel says that an angel shut the mouths of the lions, curve your clawlike fingers down to the thumb and keep quiet.
3. Every time "God" or "prayer" is mentioned, fold both hands in prayer position and bow your head.

In the Lions' Den

One child represents Daniel. All others are lions. The lions stand in a circle around Daniel, holding hands. Daniel tries to get out of the circle, but the lions try to keep him or her by closing any gap where he or she tries to escape. Daniel must quickly try one after another. The lions must keep holding hands and may not take hold of Daniel or strike him or her. (Remember, God did not let the lions hurt Daniel.) When Daniel escapes, he or she chooses the next person to be Daniel.

In the Middle of the Den

Words by Phyllis Michael; Music by Helen Friesen

This song is a lot of fun for the children to sing to remember the story of Daniel.

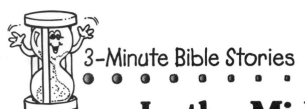

In the mid-dle of the den! In the mid-dle of the den! Yes, Dan - i - el
In the mid-dle of the den! In the mid-dle of the den! Well, Dan - i - el
In the mid-dle of the den! In the mid-dle of the den! God heard him

stood in the mid-dle of the den with big li -ons all a- round, hun-gry
prayed in the mid-dle of the den with those li -ons all a- round, hun-gry
pray in the mid-dle of the den with those li -ons all a- round, hun-gry

li -ons all a- round, Brave Dan -i -el stood in the mid-dle of the
li -ons all a- round, Brave Dan -i -el prayed in the mid-dle of the
li -ons all a- round, And God kept him safe in the mid-dle of the

den.
den.
den.

Chorus

God kept him safe! God kept him safe! Safe all right!

Jonah and the Big Fish

Jonah 1:1–3:3

Jonah was a prophet of God. God told him to go to the wicked city of Nineveh and preach God's Word to them. Jonah did not want to go to some sinful foreign city and preach, so he decided to run away! He went down to Joppa, which was on the seacoast. He found a ship that would take him far away from Nineveh and God—or so Jonah thought.

The ship with Jonah on board sailed out into a calm sea. Then God sent a great wind and storm that was about to break up the ship. The sailors were afraid and called out to their gods to save them. Jonah was below the deck, sound asleep. The captain went to him and asked him to call on his God to save them. The sailors thought someone on board had caused this disaster. They decided it must be Jonah. He had told them he was running away from his Lord. They asked him what they could do to make the sea calm again. Jonah said, "Throw me overboard." The sailors did not want to do that! They tried to get control of the ship, but nothing helped. They would all die if they did not do as Jonah said, so they finally threw him into the raging sea. It immediately became calm.

The ship sailed away, leaving Jonah bobbing in the water. As the ship went out of sight, God sent a great fish which swallowed Jonah. For three days and nights, Jonah was inside that fish. It was dark and wet and frightening. Jonah did a very good thing—he prayed. On the third day, God told the great fish to spit Jonah up on dry land. For the second time, God told Jonah to go to Nineveh. This time, Jonah obeyed the Word of the Lord.

Jonah Learns to Listen

Have the children sing this song to the tune of "Twinkle, Twinkle, Little Star" while doing the motions.

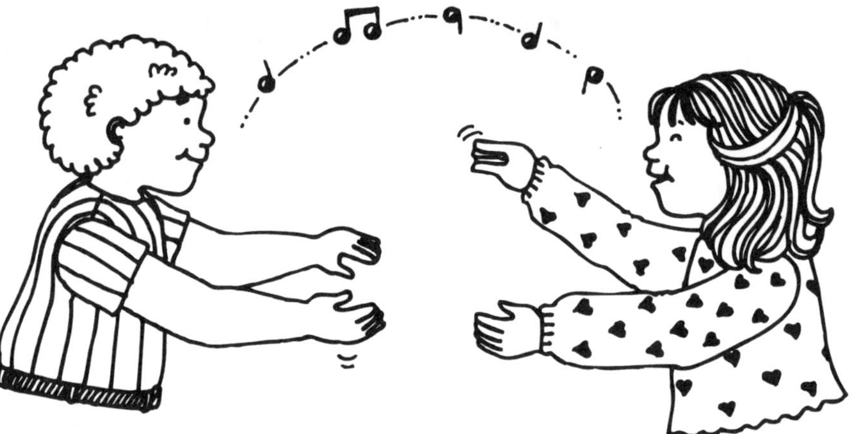

Jonah heard what God did say,	*(Cup hand over ear.)*
But he tried to run away.	*(Shake head.)*
He did not listen to his Lord.	*(Continue shaking head.)*
Sailors threw him overboard.	*(Pretend to throw something heavy with both hands.)*
A great fish swallowed him down then	*(Snap hands together like a large mouth closing.)*
And brought him to the land again.	*(Spread hands in welcoming gesture.)*
Then Jonah did what God had said,	*(Nod head.)*
And Nineveh was saved instead.	*(Clasp hands over head in victory gesture.)*
Jonah learned to listen well	*(Put hand to ear again.)*
And do whatever God should tell.	*(Shake finger as if scolding.)*
We must listen and obey	*(Cup hand over ear.)*
And praise Our Father every day.	*(Put hands together and bow head as if praying.)*

The Storm at Sea

Divide the children into two lines. Give the first child in each line a doll representing Jonah. (This may be a clothespin doll or a paper doll.) Holding it in both hands, the first child passes it over his or her head (as if Jonah is on a high wave) to the next child's two hands. The second passes the doll between his or her legs (as if Jonah is in the low trough between waves) to the third person. This continues over and under until the last child gets the doll, runs to the front, and starts "Jonah" back again. The "storm" ends when one line gets all its players back into their original places. The whole class may share the prize of a package of gummy fish or fish-shaped crackers.

Sailing Away

To make boats like the one Jonah may have sailed on, have the children follow the directions below. All they need is a piece of paper and a pencil.

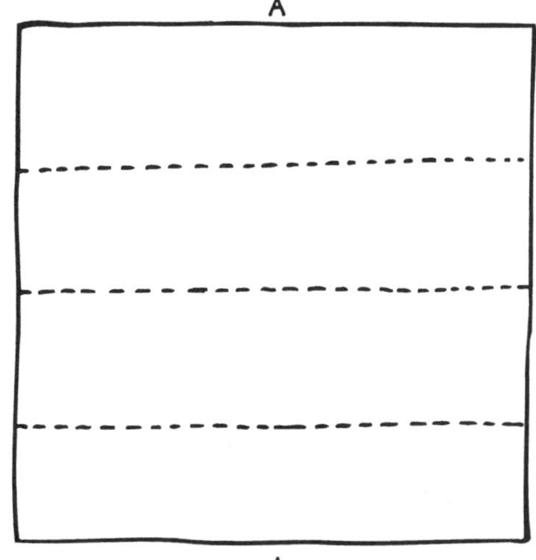

1. Fold a square piece of paper in half; then unfold. Label sides A and fold toward center.

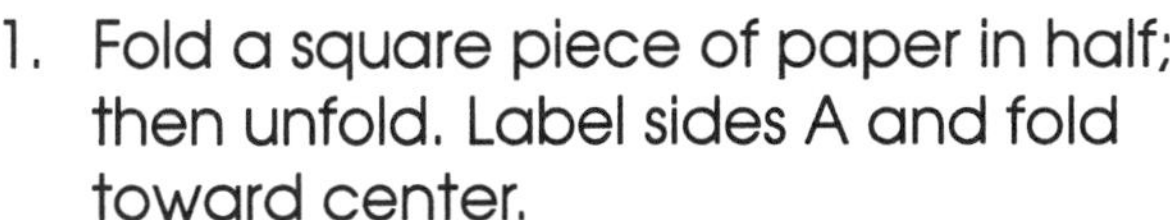

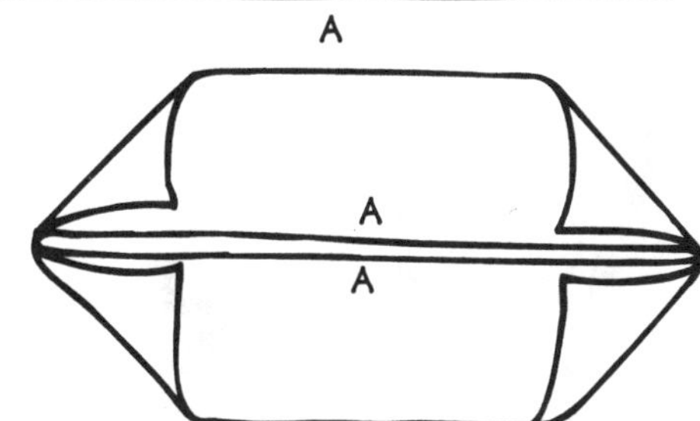

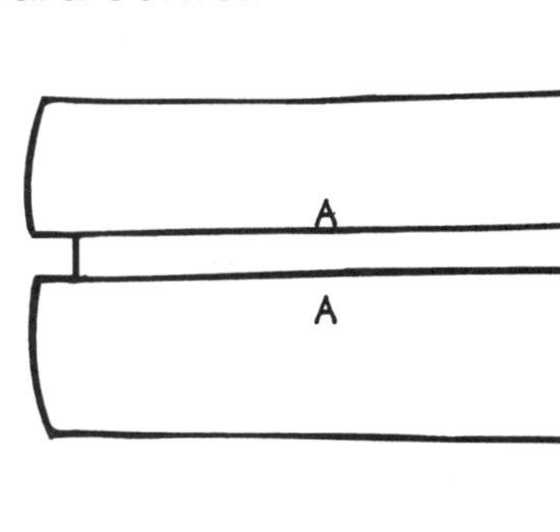

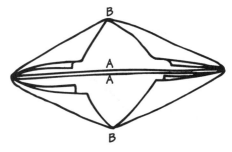

2. Fold end flaps toward center.
3. Fold again.

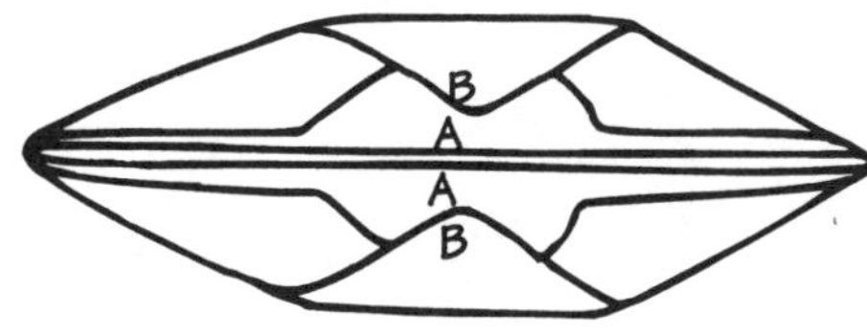

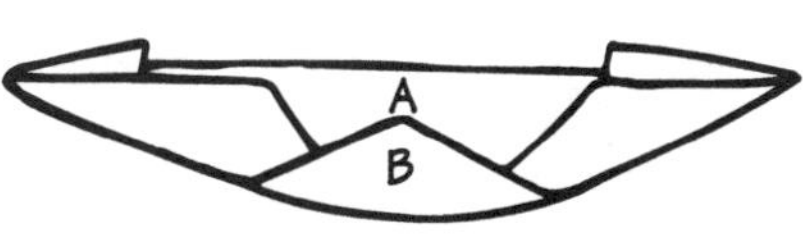

4. Label points B and fold toward center.
5. Fold paper back in half on center fold.

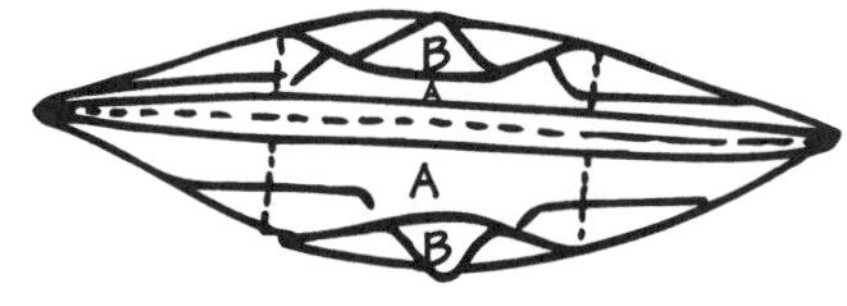

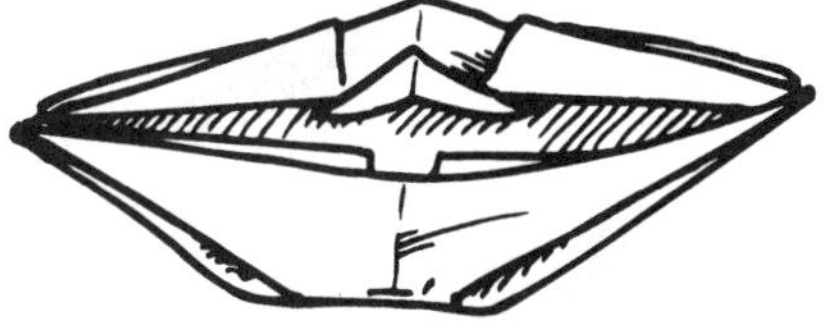

6. Take hold of the areas marked A. Pull outward slightly, holding points B, and turn inside out.
7. Smooth out with your fingers to make the boat sit evenly on a flat surface. Erase the A and B pencil marks.

Jonah Mobile

These mobiles are cute reminders for the children that we need to listen to God and do what He says.

Materials:
copies of the patterns below, construction paper, glue, scissors, pencil, thread

Directions:
Give each child a copy of the patterns. Help the children trace the fish on black construction paper and cut it out. Next, they should trace around the figure of Jonah on another color of construction paper and cut it out. The children should place Jonah in the open center of the fish and glue a piece of thread to the back of Jonah and the upper portion of the fish as illustrated. Allow at least 6" of thread above the fish for hanging.

Cut out.

Stick Figure Theater

This is the perfect way for children to retell this well-loved Bible story!

Materials:
copies of the patterns below, craft sticks, tape, crayons

Directions:
Give each child a copy of the patterns. Have the children color, cut out, and attach them to craft sticks. Let the children use them to act out the story of "Jonah and the Big Fish." Encourage the children to include this Bible verse in their stories:

But the Lord provided a great fish to swallow Jonah, and Jonah was inside the fish three days and three nights.

(Jonah 1:17)

An Angel Visits Mary

Luke 1:26–38

Mary was a young woman who lived in the town of Nazareth. One day, she had an important visitor—the angel Gabriel. *"Greetings, you who are highly favored! The Lord is with you,"* (Luke 1:28) he said.

Mary was surprised and troubled at this greeting given to her by an angel of God. She wondered what it could mean.

Gabriel went on, *"Do not be afraid, Mary, you have found favor with God. You will be with child and give birth to a son, and you are to give him the name Jesus. He will be great and will be called the Son of the Most High. The Lord God will give him the throne of his father David, and he will reign over the house of Jacob forever; his kingdom will never end."* (Luke 1:30–33)

Mary wondered, "How can this be?" for she had no husband.

The angel told Mary that God would be the baby's father. Then Gabriel told her that her cousin Elizabeth, in her old age, was also expecting a son, for nothing is impossible with God.

Mary smiled and said, "I am the servant of the Lord. May it be as you have said."

Gabriel left, and Mary had much to think about.

Angel Craft

This angel is fun to make and can be taken home to sit in the children's rooms.

Materials:

copies of the pattern below
markers or crayons
scissors
glue

Directions:

1. Have the children color the angel and cut it out on the bold lines.
2. Help the children apply glue on the tab.
3. Tell the children to roll the skirt area to fasten into a cone shape.

Apply glue here.

The Savior Is Born

Luke 1:26–38; 2:1–20; Matthew 1:18–24

At first, Joseph was upset at the news that Mary was expecting a child. Then an angel of the Lord appeared to him in a dream. The angel said, "Joseph, son of David, do not be afraid to take Mary home as your wife. She will give birth to a son, and you are to give Him the name Jesus, because He will save His people from their sins."

When Joseph woke up, he did what the angel of the Lord had commanded him and took Mary to be his wife.

At that time, the ruler of the Roman Empire issued a decree that a census should be taken of all people. Joseph and Mary left Nazareth and traveled to Bethlehem to be counted.

The trip down the long, dusty, dirt path was bumpy. Mary must have been uncomfortable as she rode on the donkey's back.

"Is the time near for the child to be born?" asked Joseph. "I'm afraid Bethlehem is so full of people, there may be nowhere to stay."

They stopped at each inn along the way. The innkeepers shook their heads and said, "Sorry, there isn't a room left in the entire city."

Finally, a kind man said they could stay in a nearby stable. That night, Mary gave birth to a baby boy. She named Him Jesus. She wrapped the tiny child in cloth and laid Him in a bed of straw.

In a nearby field, there were shepherds keeping watch over their flocks. An angel of the Lord appeared to them. "Do not be afraid," the angel assured them. "I'm here to tell you some wonderful news. It's news for all people. Today in the town of David, a Savior has been born. He is Christ the Lord. You will know Him by this sign: You will find a baby wrapped in cloths and lying in a manger." Suddenly, there were many angels in the sky, praising God.

When the angels disappeared, the shepherds said, *"Let's go to Bethlehem and see this thing that has happened, which the Lord has told us about."* (Luke 2:15) They hurried off and found Mary and Joseph and the baby lying in a manger.

Once the shepherds saw the tiny baby lying so peacefully in the hay, they praised God. Then they left and went to tell others the good news about the newborn child and what the angel had said. All who heard what the shepherds said were amazed.

Nativity Scene

Let the children make this nativity scene to use to retell the story of our Lord's birth.

Materials:
copies of the patterns shown, markers or crayons, scissors, glue

Directions:

1. Tell the children to color the pictures and cut them out on the bold lines.
2. Tell them to fold on the dotted lines.
3. Next, the children should glue the top of the roof as shown and then glue the Mary and Joseph figures in the middle.

Finished picture

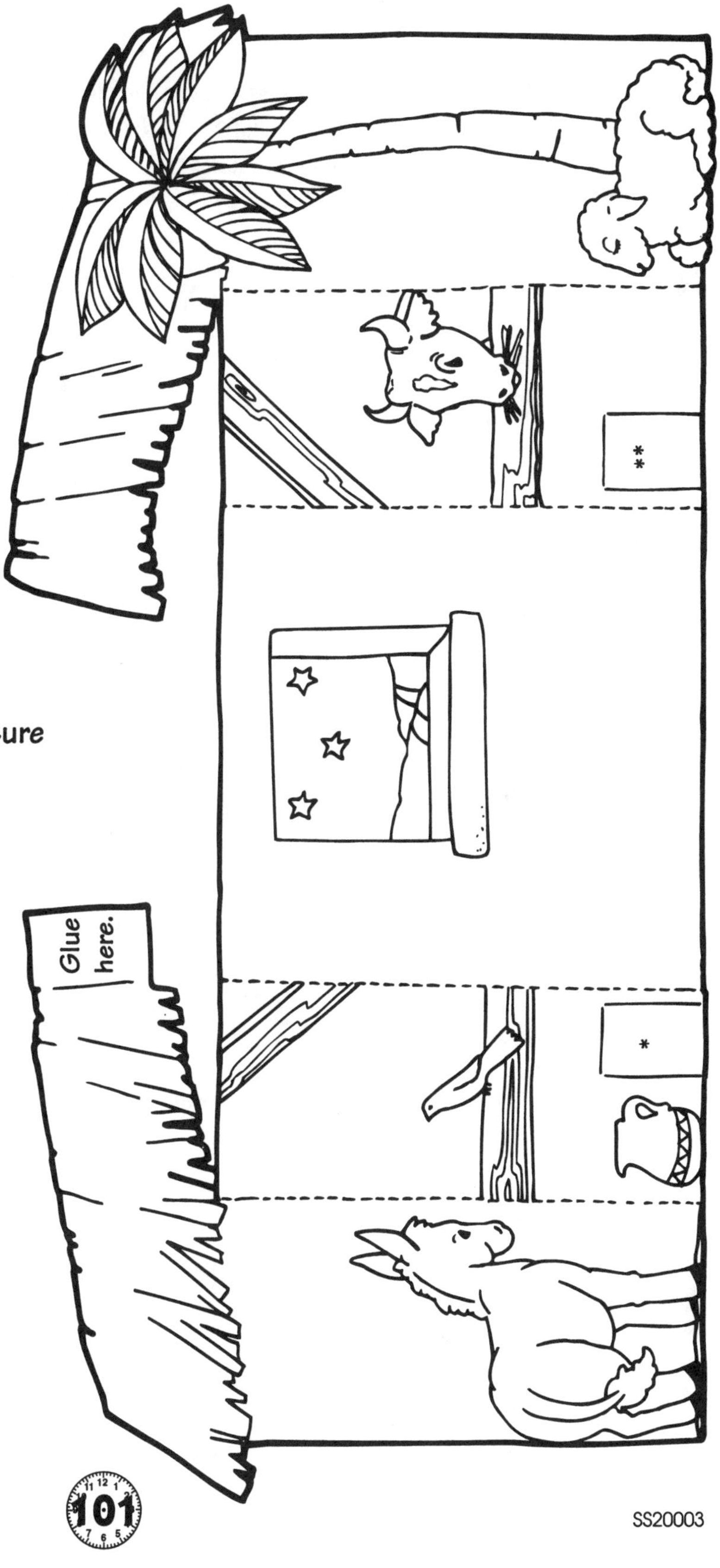

Glue here.

Advent Wreath

An advent wreath is a wonderful way to prepare the children for Christ's birth.

To make an Advent wreath, press four candles into a Styrofoam™ wreath so they stand an equal distance from each other. Glue silk or plastic greenery around the base of the wreath. Make copies of the patterns below and on page 103 the children can color and cut out to help retell the story of Jesus' birth.

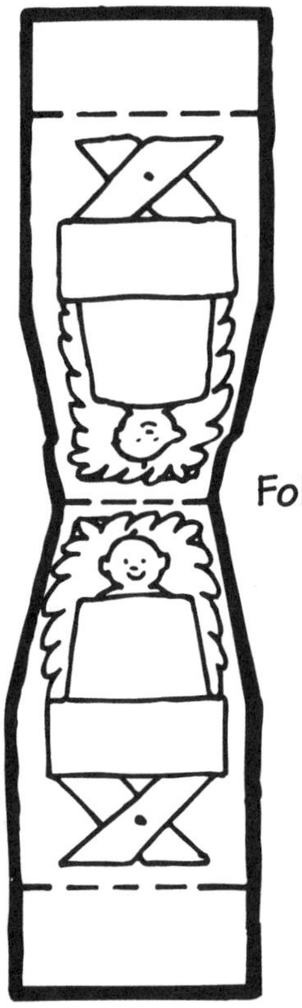

Fold.

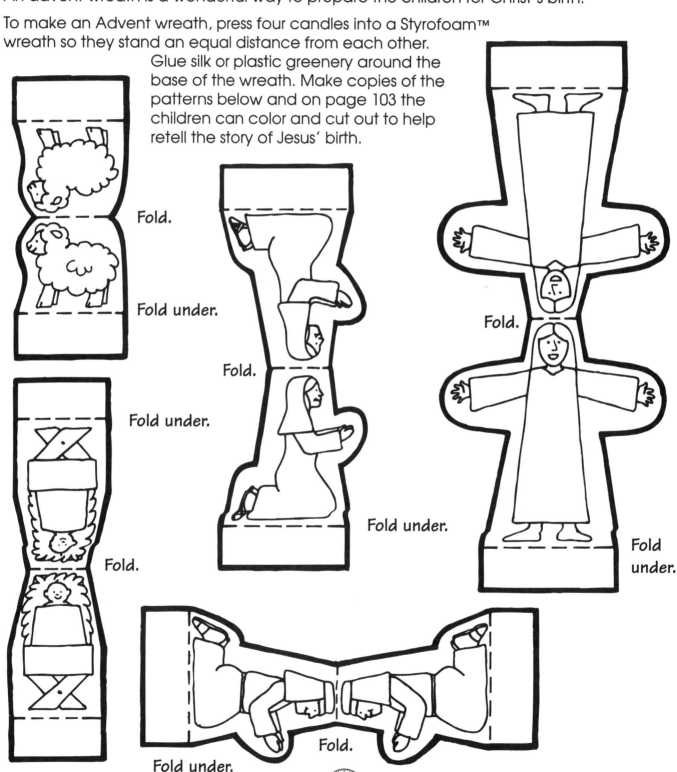

Fold under.

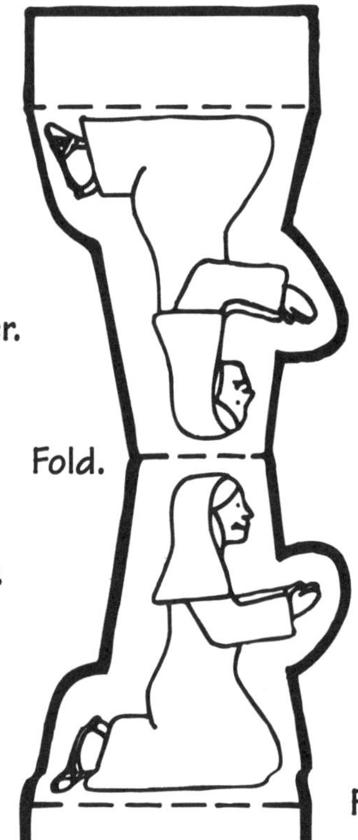

Fold.

Fold under.

Fold.

Fold under.

Fold under.

Fold.

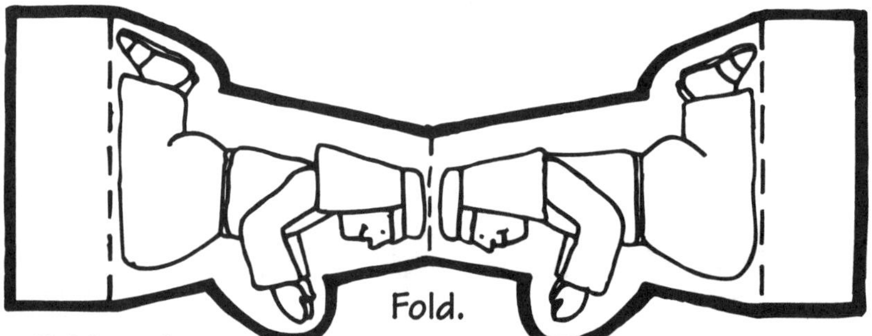

Fold under.

Fold.

Fold under.

Patterns

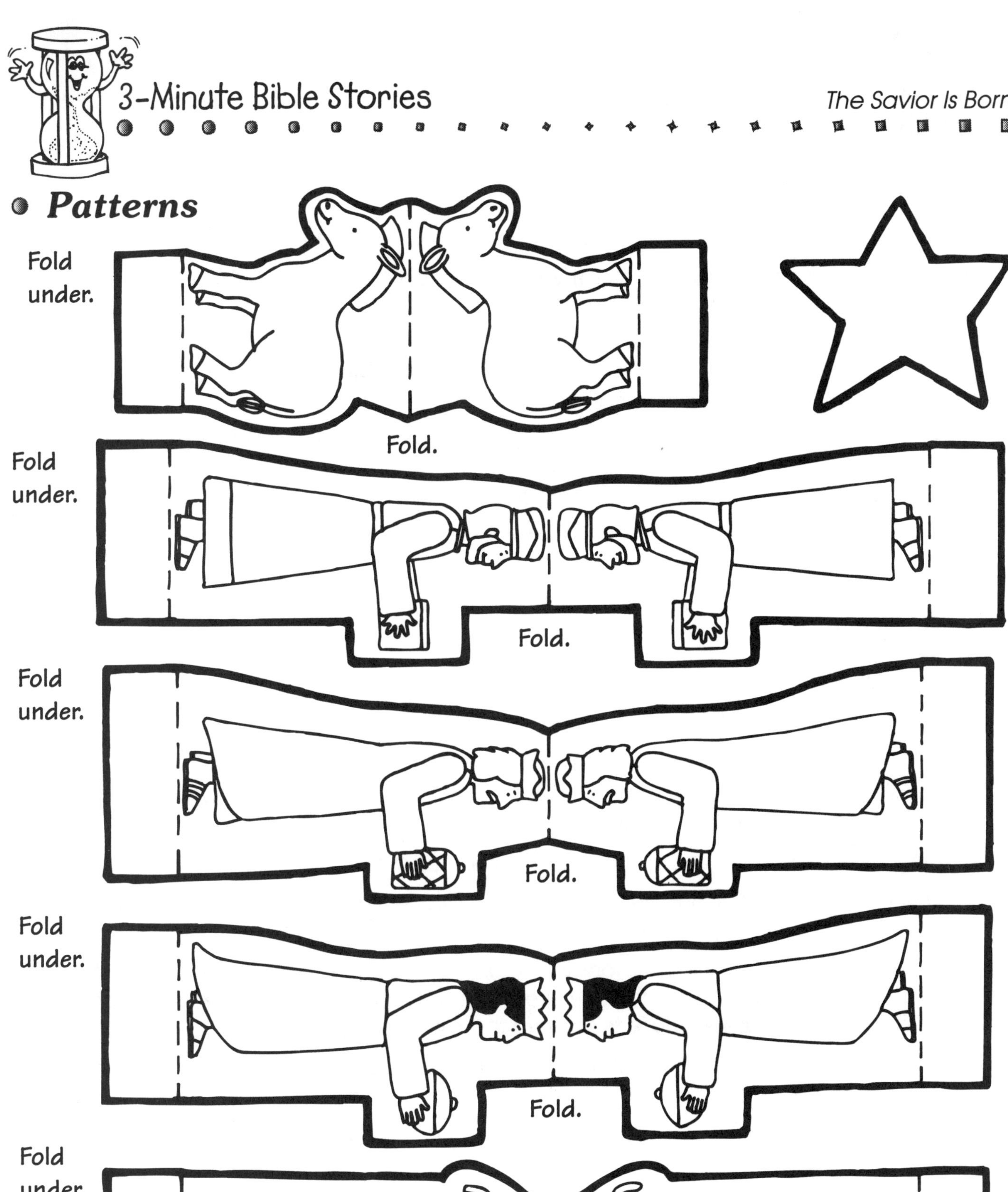
Fold under.
Fold.
Fold under.
Fold.
Fold under.
Fold.
Fold under.
Fold.
Fold under.
Fold.

Advent Activities

Below is a list of fun activities the children can do to celebrate Advent.

1. Make an Advent wreath (follow the directions on page 102). Light one candle on the wreath. Read Romans 13:11–12.
2. Make a family tree by tracing handprints on green construction paper. Roll up the fingers slightly. Line up the hands in the shape of a tree and glue them on posterboard. Add a gold star on top.
3. Make personalized Christmas balls using construction paper. Write each family member's name in glitter on a construction paper circle. Tie a bow with ribbon or yarn and glue it onto the family handprint tree.
4. Cover a large Styrofoam™ ball with mistletoe. Hang it above your door. Give people kisses of peace as they enter your home.
5. Cut the letters "HAPPY BIRTHDAY, JESUS" from colorful magazine pages. Hang them in the window.
6. Look at last year's Christmas cards. Pray for those who sent them.
7. Light the second candle on the Advent wreath. Read Matthew 3:3.
8. Make Christmas cards for friends and family.
9. Go shopping together for a Christmas tree. Enjoy hot apple cider while sharing your favorite thing about Christmas.
10. Sing Christmas songs as you bake Christmas goodies for friends.
11. Talk about the important gifts you have received. Visit a friend in need, sharing some of your homemade goodies.
12. Make Christmas tree decorations by cutting out scenes from last year's Christmas cards. Punch a hole in the top and tie each with a piece of yarn. As this year's Christmas cards arrive, share them with the family each evening.
13. Light the third candle on the Advent wreath. String popcorn for a Christmas tree decoration.
14. Talk about memories of past Christmases. Paint a shoebox to be used for a Nativity scene.
15. Light the fourth candle on the Advent wreath. Join hands and sing "Happy Birthday" to Jesus.
16. Before opening Christmas gifts, have a short worship and prayer time.
17. After Christmas is over, write a thank-you note to God.

A Star Leads the Way

Matthew 2:1–12

King Herod ruled in the land of Judea. He was a cruel and wicked man. One day, Magi appeared at his court. These wise and educated men were from a land in the east. The king wondered what had brought them to his country.

The Magi asked, *"Where is the one who has been born king of the Jews? We saw his star in the east and have come to worship him."* (Matthew 2:2)

These words upset King Herod. He was king and no one else. He called his priests and teachers of the Law and asked them where the king of the Jews was to be born. They replied that the Scriptures said it would be Bethlehem.

Herod met with the Magi. He told them, *"Go and make a careful search for the child. As soon as you find him, report to me, so that I too may go and worship him."* (Matthew 2:8)

The Magi did not know how wicked King Herod was. They did not realize that he planned to kill the child. They left Jerusalem and began to follow the star once again.

They traveled for many days as the star went ahead of them. Then as they neared the town of Bethlehem, the star stopped. It shone over the house where the child lived. The Magi were overjoyed! The star had led them to the new king!

They entered the house and saw Mary with the child. They bowed down and worshipped Him. Then they gave Him gifts of gold, incense, and myrrh. These were gifts fit for a king! That night, God spoke to the Magi in a dream and warned them not to go back to Herod but to return to their country another way. They obeyed God's warning.

The Star of Bethlehem

This star will help the children remember what the Magi followed to find baby Jesus.

Materials:
copies of the patterns on this page, markers or crayons, scissors, hole punch, glue, thread or yarn

Directions:

1. Have the children color the points of the star pattern yellow and cut it out on the bold lines.
2. Tell them to fold on the dotted lines.
3. Help the children apply glue on the tab and fasten to area *. Then they should apply glue behind the points and bend the points back to fasten.
4. Tell each child to cut out the message pentagon pattern and glue it on the front of the star.
5. Finally, they punch a hole in the star point where the black dot is and insert a 10" piece of thread to tie into a loop. Hang the stars around the room.

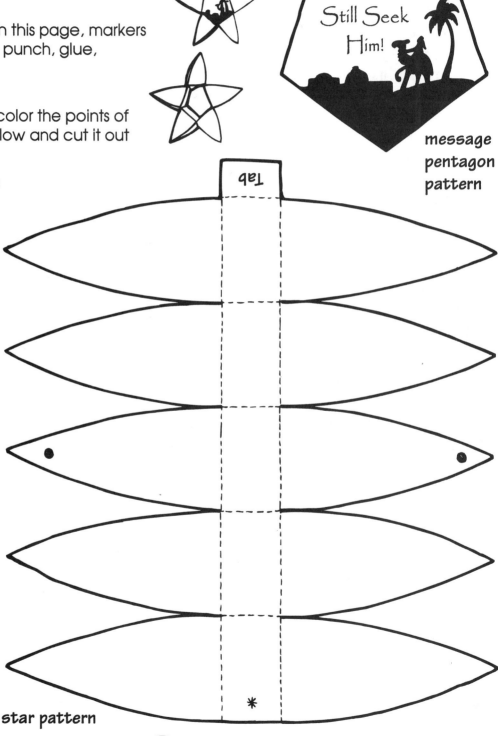

Wise Men Still Seek Him!

message pentagon pattern

Tab

*

star pattern

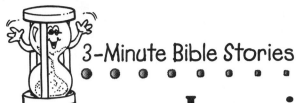

Jesus in the Temple

Luke 2:41–52

Every spring, Mary and Joseph went to Jerusalem for the celebration of the Passover (a special festival held in memory of the Israelites' escape from slavery in Egypt). When He was old enough, they took Jesus with them. A lot of their friends and relatives were going, too. Some people walked, and some rode donkeys, but they all had a good time on the way. They talked and told stories and sang psalms.

Mary and Joseph were in Jerusalem two or three days. After the celebration was over, they started back to Nazareth. On the way home, Mary and Joseph realized that Jesus was not with them, but they thought He was with some of His cousins in the crowd.

That evening, when Jesus did not arrive for supper, Mary and Joseph were worried. They went through the crowd, asking all their friends and relatives if Jesus was with them. Nobody had seen Him.

The next morning when everybody else went on towards Nazareth, Mary and Joseph left the crowd. They went back to Jerusalem to try to find Jesus. They spent three days looking and asking people along the way and in the city. They were getting very worried and upset.

At last they found Him, sitting in one of the temple courtyards, asking the teachers questions and talking with them. People who heard Him said afterwards that they were amazed at this boy's questions and answers.

Jesus in the Temple continued

As soon as she could get to Him, Mary said to Jesus, "My son, why have You treated us like this? You knew it was time to be going home. Your father and I have been worried. We have been looking everywhere for You."

Jesus asked them: "Why have you been searching for me? Didn't you know I would be here in my Father's house?"

Mary and Joseph did not really understand what He meant, but Mary kept thinking about what He had said.

Jesus went with Mary and Joseph back to Nazareth. He was twelve years old and beginning to grow up. The Bible says He *grew in wisdom and stature* (Luke 2:52)—that means His mind was growing and learning to think more, and His body was growing taller and stronger. The Bible also says He grew "in favor with God and man." That means He did what God wanted Him to do, and everybody liked Him. Jesus was growing in every way.

His Father's House

Let the children make this church to remind them where Mary and Joseph found Jesus.

Materials:
copies of the patterns shown, scissors, glue, crayons

Directions:

1. Have the children color the inside and outside of their churches.
2. Next, the children should cut out their churches on the bold lines, including the center and the top of the door.
3. Show the children how to glue pattern A behind the door.
4. The children can fold the door on the dotted lines and open it to see inside.

pattern A

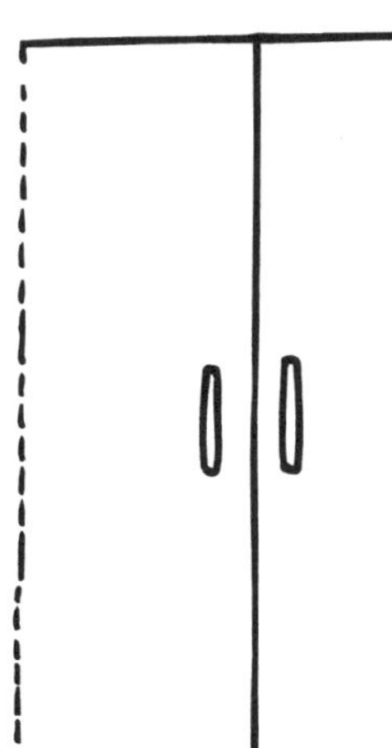

He Grew in Wisdom and Stature

What the Bible says about how Jesus grew should be true for all of us who are still growing. Say the chant below together to help you remember it. Ask for a volunteer to read the solo lines. Have the rest of the group speak the chorus lines.

Solo: When Jesus was just a little boy,

Chorus: He grew in wisdom and stature
And in favor with God and man.

Solo: When Jesus was a bigger boy,

Chorus: He grew in wisdom and stature
And in favor with God and man.

Solo: Now Jesus wants everyone of us blessed

Chorus: As we grow in wisdom and stature
And in favor with God and man.

Solo: So we promise that we will do our best

Chorus: To grow in wisdom and stature
And in favor with God and man.

Jesus Is Missing

Mary or Joseph is trying to find Jesus to take Him home. Seat half of the children in a circle of chairs, leaving one chair empty. The rest of the children stand, one behind each chair, including the empty one left for their son. All those standing must have their hands clasped behind them.

Whoever stands behind the empty chair (either "Mary" or "Joseph") tries to get his or her "son" to sit there. He or she looks around the circle and suddenly says to one of the seated children, "Come." That child tries to run to the empty chair, but the child behind him or her grabs his or her shoulders and tries to hold him or her in the chair. If the standing child succeeds, "Joseph" or "Mary" tries someone else. If the standing child loses the seated child, he or she becomes Joseph or Mary and tries to bring someone else to the empty chair.

The Boy Jesus in the Temple

This play is fun for the children to act out and put on for parents and other children.

Cast of characters:

Narrator
Jesus
Mary
Joseph
Friends of Mary and Joseph
Townspeople
Wise teachers

Narrator: The time has come for Jesus to go to the big city and see the temple.

Mary: Come with us, Jesus, to Jerusalem.

Jesus: I would love to go to Jerusalem and see the temple!

Narrator: It was a long walk to Jerusalem. *(Mary, Joseph, Jesus, and friends walk.)*

Jesus: *(Looking around the temple)* Oh, how big the temple is, and how beautiful!

Narrator: Jesus sat among the wise teachers and listened to them speak of God. How surprised the teachers were when they heard the things Jesus knew.

Teacher 1: How wise this young boy is!

Teacher 2: He knows so many things about God's Word!

Narrator: When they started home, Mary and Joseph thought Jesus was with them, walking with His friends. When time passed and Jesus did not come to them, they began to worry.

Joseph: Mary, have you seen Jesus? He did not eat with us or sleep with us. Is He with some friends?

Mary: Oh my! Where can He be? *(to friends)* Have you seen our son, Jesus? We cannot find Him.

The Boy Jesus . . . continued

Joseph: We must look for Him until we find Him. We shall go back to Jerusalem and search for Him there.

Narrator: Mary and Joseph were very worried as they hurried back to Jerusalem. When they arrived, they were tired and afraid. They began stopping people in the streets and knocking on doors.

Joseph: *(Knocking on door)* Have you seen a boy, about twelve years old, this high . . . ?

Townsperson: No, I have seen no one.

Mary: *(Knocking on door)* Have you seen a boy? He is our son . . .

Townsperson: I was at the temple today. There is a boy there—a very wise boy talking about heaven and earth.

Narrator: Mary and Joseph rushed to the temple, praying that Jesus would be there. When they arrived, they found their son sitting with the wise teachers.

Mary: Jesus, why did You do this? We have looked everywhere for You.

Joseph: When we could not find You, we thought You were lost.

Mary: We were so worried about You.

Jesus: God is My Father. I was doing His work. Didn't you know that I had to be here in My Father's house?

God is My Father.
I was doing His work.

Narrator: Then Jesus left the temple. He went home with Mary and Joseph. Jesus continued to grow in wisdom. Mary often thought about her son, Jesus. She knew He was very special.

Mary: I will always remember how glad Jesus was to hear the Word of God in the temple.

A Dove From Heaven

Matthew 3:1–17

Jesus' cousin John was a popular preacher. He spoke to people in the Desert of Judea. John wore camel hair clothes and ate locusts and honey. He was a strange man, but people listened to his powerful message about repenting for their sins because the kingdom was near. He baptized many people in the Jordan River, and it was there that Jesus came to begin His work for God.

John was telling the people, "I baptize with water but one will come after me who is more powerful. I am not fit to even carry His sandals."

Then Jesus came to the Jordan River and told John He wanted to be baptized. John was amazed. Jesus should baptize him!

Jesus said, *"It is proper for us to do this to fulfill all righteousness."* (Matthew 3:15)

Hearing these words, John agreed. He baptized Jesus Christ, the Son of God, in the Jordan River. As Jesus came up out of the water, heaven opened and the Spirit of God came down in the form of a dove.

The dove came to rest on Jesus and a voice from heaven said, *"This is my Son, whom I love; with him I am well pleased."* (Matthew 3:17)

The dove returned to heaven, then Jesus left the Jordan River and went out into the desert.

Where Is John?

Sing this variation of the old familiar song, "Where Is Thumbkin?" Use markers to draw a face on each of your thumbs and fingers.

Put your hands behind your back. Bring out your right thumb for John as you sing the second line of the first stanza. Bring out your left thumb for Jesus as you sing the second line of the second stanza.

On the second line of the last stanza, wiggle the rest of your fingers for the people. Bring the fingers together and fold your hands as if praying for the final line, "Praise to God."

Where is John? Where is John?
Here I am. Here I am.
Near the Jordan River,
Near the Jordan River,
Baptizing. Baptizing.

Where is Jesus? Where is Jesus?
Here I am. Here I am.
Coming to the river,
Coming to the river,
Baptize Me. Baptize Me.

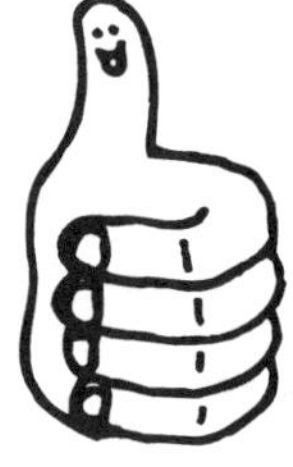

Where are the people? Where are the people?
Here we are. Here we are.
Coming to the river,
Coming to the river,
Praise to God. Praise to God.

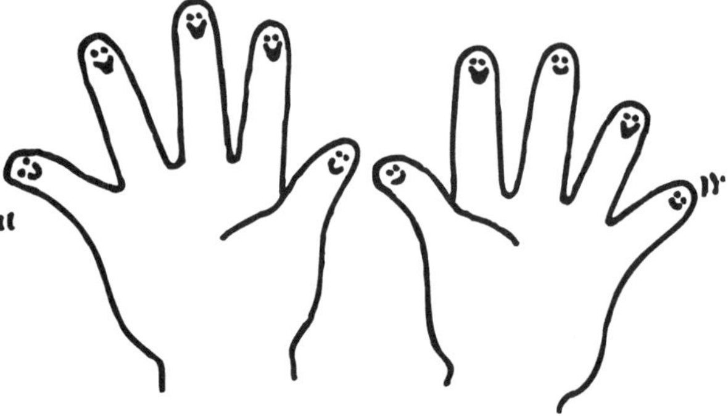

Sun Catcher Fun

This is a fun craft for children to make to help them remember to follow Jesus as John the Baptist did.

Materials:
copies of the pattern below, vegetable or salad oil, rags or paper towels, crayons, scissors, string, hole punch

Directions:
Tell the children to color the pattern and cut it out. They should use bright colors and press firmly with their crayons to produce even, solid colors. Help the children use an old rag or paper towel to spread a small amount of oil over their entire pictures. Then they use a clean rag or towel to rub off the excess oil. Next, help them use a hole punch to make a hole at the top, where indicated. A short length of string can then be inserted to form a loop for hanging.

Have the children memorize this Bible verse to help them with the activity below:

And a voice from heaven said, "This is my Son, whom I love; with him I am well pleased." (Matthew 3:17)

Dove Search

Materials:

copies of the dove pattern below, construction paper, tape

Directions:

Cut out 19 doves from construction paper using the pattern. On each dove, print one word from the Bible verse Matthew 3:17. Tape the doves around the room. Have the children take turns finding the dove with the word from the verse that you call out. When all 19 doves have been found, ask children to tape them in the correct order on a wall or bulletin board. Read the completed verse together.

Fishers of Men

Luke 5:1–11

Sometimes Jesus taught people in the synagogues of the villages where He went. Other times, He talked to people out in the countryside. After He became well-known, He had to teach outdoors because the crowds of people who wanted to hear Him were too big to get in a building.

One day, Jesus was standing by the Sea of Galilee talking to people. Everybody wanted to get close to Him. Some wanted to hear what He was saying; others wanted to be healed. The trouble was, the more they crowded close to Him, the harder it was to make all of them hear.

Then He noticed two boats nearby at the edge of the water. Their owners were not in them. They were on the beach mending their fishing nets. Jesus didn't think they would mind letting Him use one of their boats for a little while. He stepped into one of the boats and pushed it out into the water. Nobody else could get in, but everybody could see and hear Him.

When He had finished talking, Jesus wanted to do something for Simon to thank him for the use of his boat. (Simon, who was also called Peter, was one of the fishermen mending his nets.) Jesus said to him, "Pull out into deeper water and let down your nets for a load of fish."

Simon Peter shook his head and said, "Master, we have worked all night and haven't caught any." Then he changed his mind. He said, "Still, if You say so, I'll try again."

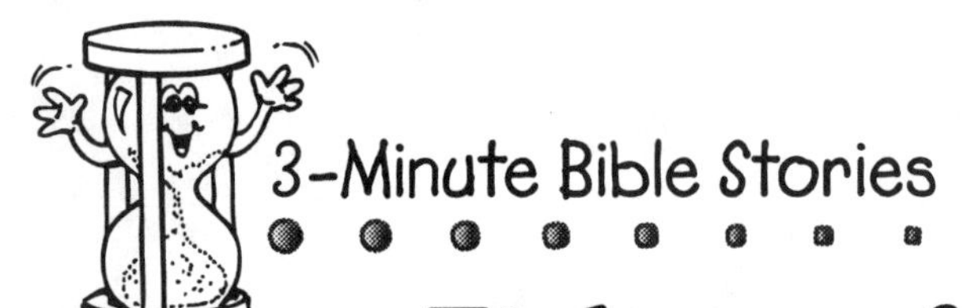

Fishers of Men continued

He and his helpers rowed the boat out a little ways. Then they threw out the nets. They caught so many fish that the nets began to break. Simon called to the other fishermen, "Bring the second boat!" His friends brought the boat as fast as they could and helped pull the nets in. The two boats were filled so full they were almost ready to sink!

Simon Peter bowed to Jesus and told Him to go away. He said Jesus was too wonderful to be with a sinner such as he.

Jesus told him, "Don't worry. From now on you will not catch just fish, you will fish for men."

Simon Peter and his friends pulled their boats in to shore where they left them to follow Jesus. From then on, they were fishers of men, just as Jesus had told them. They were the first disciples.

The disciples told many people about Jesus. Their stories of Jesus caught people's attention just the way they had caught fish before. The disciples now "caught" people for Jesus.

Have the children memorize this Bible verse and illustrate it on sheets of paper:

"Come, follow me," Jesus said, "and I will make you fishers of men." (Matthew 4:19)

Gone Fishing

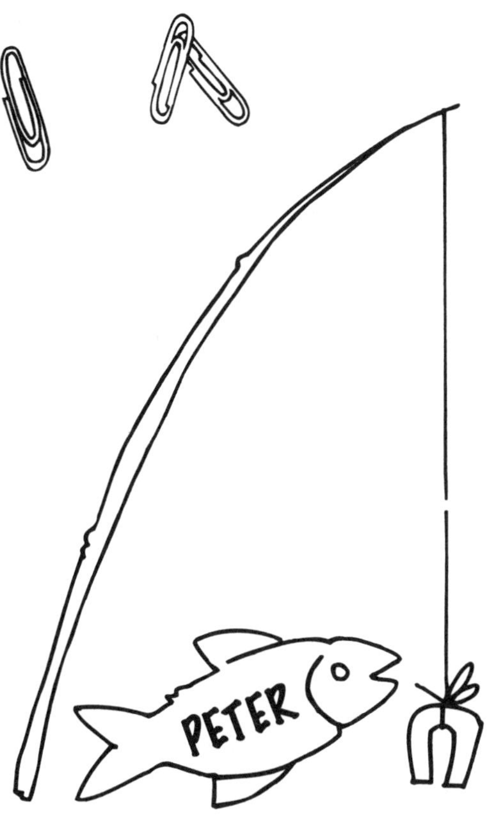

Materials:

copies of the fish pattern on page 122
a stick with string and a magnet
paper clips

Directions:

1. Using the pattern, cut out 12 fish. Print the name of a disciple on each of them (Simon Peter, Andrew, James, John, Philip, Bartholomew, Thomas, Matthew, James, Thaddaeus, Simon, Judas Iscariot).
2. Attach paper clips to the fish. Scatter them on the floor with the names of the disciples right side up.
3. Give a child the pole and tell him or her to "catch" the fish that has the name of the disciple described in the clue you give.

   Clues:

   - the brother of John (James)
   - the beloved disciple (John)
   - the tax collector (Matthew)
   - the son of Alphaeus (James)
   - the disciple with the longest name (Bartholomew)
   - the disciple whose name has nine letters in it (Thaddaeus)
   - the disciple who walked on water (Simon Peter)
   - the brother of Peter (Andrew)
   - the one who betrayed Jesus (Judas Iscariot)
   - the one called the Zealot (Simon)
   - the one who was a doubter (Thomas)
   - the one who told Nathanael about Jesus (Philip)
4. If a child "catches" the wrong fish, he or she must throw it back and give someone else a turn. Continue until all the fish are caught.

Catching the Fish

Choose one child to be a fish; all the others are fishermen. The fish carries a package of fish-shaped crackers. The fishermen join hands in a long line. Their objective is to get the first and last fishermen to join hands, making a circular "net" with the fish inside the circle. The fish tries to avoid being surrounded. When he or she is finally encircled, he or she shares the crackers with the fishermen who caught him or her.

Fishers of Men

With motions, sing this song to the tune of "This Old Man."

Fishermen	
Cast their net,	*(Broad arm motion.)*
But the fish they could not get.	*(Shake head.)*
Hauled hard, threw their nets—	*(Pulling, then throwing motions.)*
Anywhere would do.	*(Shrug.)*
Caught no fish	*(Shake head and move hands in front*
The whole night through.	*of body, palms down.)*
Jesus called,	*(Hand to side of mouth.)*
"Come to Me.	*(Beckon.)*
Leave your boats there by the sea.	*(Point with right arm.)*
Pray and show your faith	*(Fold hands together; look up to heaven.)*
Anyway you wish.	*(Hands, palms up, in front; shrug.)*
You will catch	*(Arms in wide inclusive gesture.)*
More men than fish."	

3-D Fish

These fish can be made and hung on a bulletin board or on the wall, or they can be used to let the children have fun "fishing."

Materials:

copies of the fish pattern on page 122
butcher paper
paper clips
colored construction paper
scrap paper
marker
crayons
magnet
stapler (optional)
stick
glue
yarn
scissors

Directions:

1. Give each child a copy of the large fish shape on page 122.
2. Help the children use crayons to lightly trace the fish on construction paper.
3. Help them add a second sheet and cut two fish out.
4. Show the children how to glue the sides together, leaving a 6" opening near the back end.
5. Help the children stuff their fish with scrap paper and glue the openings closed. (A few staples may be needed to close the openings.)
6. Tell the children to attach a paper clip to the top of their fish.

Color a large sheet of butcher paper blue; then lay it on the floor to represent the ocean. Tie a piece of yarn to a stick for a fishing pole. Attach a magnet to the end of the yarn. Toss several fish onto the butcher paper and let the children take turns trying to "catch" them.

When the "fishing" is over, print "I will make you fishers of men" across the butcher paper and hang it on the wall. (You may want to color in some seaweed and other fish.) Attach a piece of yarn to each fish and hang it from the ceiling in front of the "ocean" for a three-dimensional bulletin board. (See completed bulletin board on page 122.)

Fish Pattern

I WILL MAKE YOU FISHERS OF MEN

bulletin board

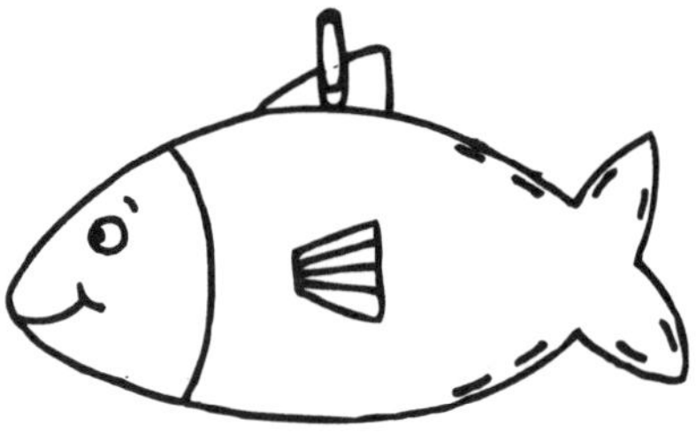

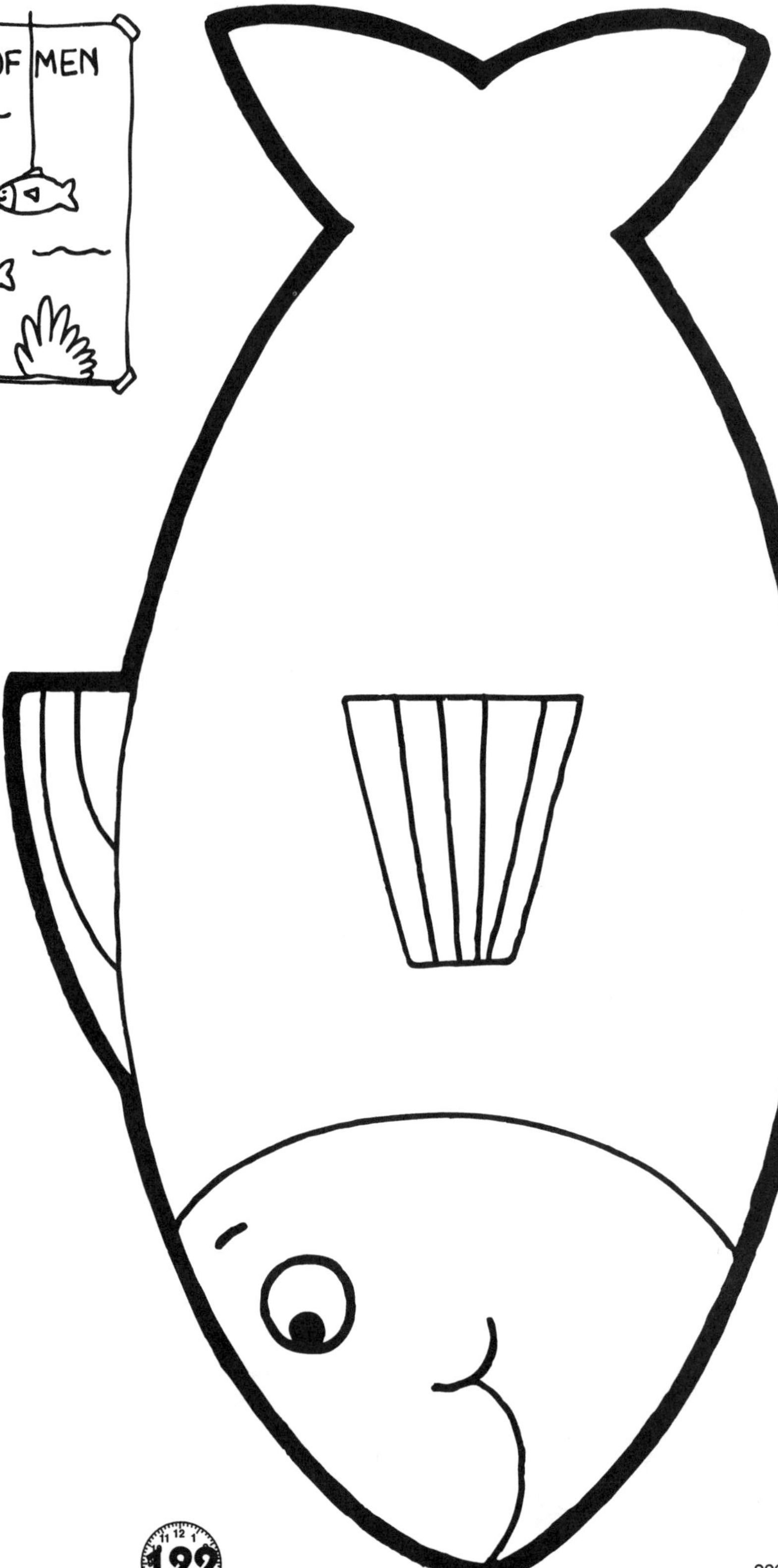

Jesus Calms the Storm

Matthew 8:23–27; Mark 4:35–41; Luke 8:22–25

It was a beautiful, quiet night. Jesus stood at the shore of the Sea of Galilee. He listened to the rippling waves gently splashing against the small boats anchored at the wharf. They rocked slightly back and forth.

Jesus was tired. He had worked hard talking to the large crowds of people that day. Men, women, and children had traveled for miles to hear Him preach God's Word and watch Him heal the sick.

Jesus called to His disciples, "Let's go over to the other side of the lake." His friends untied the boat and lifted the sails. As the soft breeze touched the cloth, the boat floated out to sea. The gentle rocking soothed Jesus. He went to the back of the boat and quickly fell asleep as they sailed out into the sea.

Suddenly, without warning, the sky grew dark. A large, black cloud appeared. The waves began to roll higher. Water crashed against the sides of the boat. The men yelled as they worked to bring the sails in, "We're all going to die in this storm!"

The dark clouds burst open, and rain poured down, throwing the boat farther out into the sea. The men's arms ached as they tried to row the boat to shore.

"Quickly, wake Jesus!" cried one of the disciples.

The men shouted, "Lord, save us! We're all going to die!" And Jesus woke up.

Jesus was calm as He replied, "You of little faith, why are you so afraid?" Slowly He stood and looked out on the sea. He scolded the winds and the waves. Just like a child ashamed of being naughty, the storm quieted, and the seas became calm.

The disciples gasped in amazement. "What kind of man is this?" they asked. "Even the winds and the waves obey Him!"

Storming Good Fun

Below are two activities you can do involving a poem about Jesus calming the storm. The children will enjoy both as they make beautiful pictures and practice creative dramatics skills.

Materials:

copies of the poem below
copies of the patterns on pages 125–126
construction paper (yellow, white, light blue, dark blue, and black)
scissors
glue
pencil

Directions:

Make copies of the patterns on construction paper for the children and have them cut them out. (black and white = clouds and lightning, yellow = moon, dark blue = waves)

Give each child a full sheet of light blue construction paper to use for the background. The children should fold back the top of the paper 1 ½" and fold back the bottom 1 ½". With the two edges folded back, tell the children to glue on the white cloud, moon, and waves as shown. The boat can be glued in the center.

Next, have the children unfold the top and bottom of the paper and glue the lightning, black cloud, and waves on the back of the folded pieces.

Now the poem below can be glued to the back of the picture. Help the children read the poem and open and close the folds to illustrate the story.

It was calm upon the sea.
The moon and the stars shone bright
When Jesus and His disciples
Set sail that quiet night.

Then all at once the lightning flashed!
A cloud burst overhead.
The waves began to tumble.
The men cried, "We'll all be dead!"

But Jesus called out to the storm,
"Be calm; obey My will."
The disciples stood in wonder
As the wind and waves grew still.

Storming Good Fun continued

For more poem fun, staple several large cardboard boxes together to form a boat. Have the children stand in the boxes and pretend to be the disciples on that night when Jesus calmed the sea. Practice the poem on page 124 together, having the children do the motions listed below for each verse. Choose one child to be Jesus and several others to be the disciples. Children that are not chosen for special parts may recite the poem while the others act it out.

Verse 1—"Disciples" look up at the sky and smile.

Verse 2—"Disciples" cover their heads and move boxes back and forth.

Verse 3—"Jesus" stands and points to the sky. Everything is still.

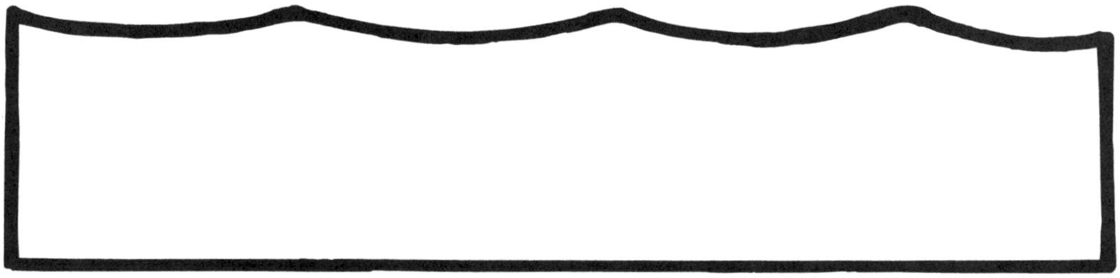

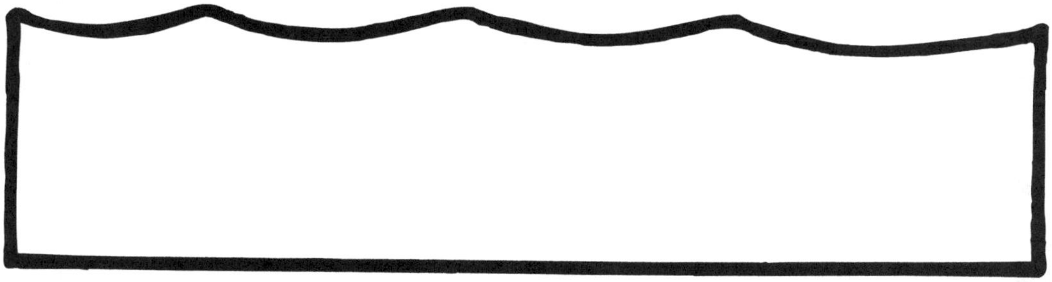

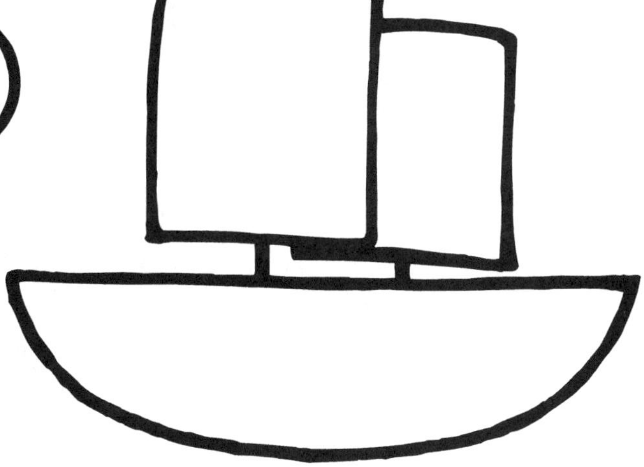

Patterns

Jesus Heals the Paralyzed Man

Luke 5:17–26

One day, Jesus was teaching in a house in Capernaum. People had come from all over Galilee and Judea to hear Him. Lawyers and Pharisees were listening. (Pharisees were Jewish religious leaders.) Such a crowd had gathered that nobody else could get near Jesus.

Some men were late getting there. They had brought a paralyzed friend to have Jesus heal him. He could not move or stand up. They were late because they had carried their friend all the way on his bed. (The beds in those days were like pads or gym mats.) Each of the friends had carried one corner of the mat with the sick man lying on it.

When they got to the house, so many people were crowded around, they could not get in. What could they do? They had carried their friend all the way from his house. They were sure Jesus would heal him if they could just get near.

Then one of the men had an idea. "Let's take some of the tiles off the roof," he said. "We can put them back afterwards. If we let the bed down through the roof, everybody will have to move to make room for it."

The others agreed. They went around to the side where the stairs led up to the flat roof. Quickly they pried up the tiles. Then carefully they lowered the bed with their friend on it right down in front of Jesus.

Jesus Heals . . . continued

Everybody else was surprised, but Jesus was pleased. He realized that they had faith enough to work hard in order to get their friend to Him. He looked down at the sick man on the mat and said, "Friend, your sins are forgiven."

Nobody had expected Him to say that. The Pharisees and the lawyers thought Jesus had no right to say it. They were thinking that only God could forgive sins.

Jesus knew what they were thinking. He wanted them to learn something they had not thought about. Because He was the Son of God, Jesus could forgive sins. He asked the people around Him, "Which is easier to say, 'Your sins are forgiven,' or 'Get up and walk'?"

Nobody answered Him. He looked down at the paralyzed man again and said, "Get up. Take your mat and go home."

At once, the paralyzed man was able to stand. He picked up the mat he had been lying on. Then he praised God for his healing. He looked around for his friends; then he went home to his family. Everybody else was praising God, too, for the wonderful healing they had seen that day.

A Sick Man's Friends

Have the children sing this song to the tune of "Hush, Little Baby."

A sick man's friends said, "We know how you feel.
We'll take you to Jesus, for He can heal.

"If you can't walk, we'll carry you instead.
We'll take your there on your very own bed.

"If we can't get to Him on the ground,
We'll take you to the rooftop and let you down.

"And He will heal and forgive your sins,
So you can stand up and walk again."

And that's what they did; Jesus healed the man.
He stood and thanked God; then home he ran.

Carrying a Sick Man

To help the children see what a difficult task the friends of the sick man undertook, try the race below.

Divide children into groups of four. Give each group a newspaper page to represent the bed. Each child takes one corner. On the bed, place a crumpled piece of tissue paper to represent the man. (This light weight will blow off if they move too fast.) At the signal, each group of four starts across the room. The children must keep their "bed" flat enough and move slowly enough that they do not spill the man from his bed, nor hold the corners so far up that he is uncomfortable in the middle. The first group that gets across the room wins. If some stairs are safely available, the four may be required to go up a few steps and let their friend down carefully before their task is done.

Five Loaves and Two Fish

Matthew 14:13–21

Jesus had gone to a quiet place to be alone, but the crowds followed Him from the towns. He had compassion on them and began to heal the sick.

The hour grew late, and the disciples came to Jesus to say that He should send the people away so they could walk to a village and buy food. The crowd numbered over 5,000!

Jesus said, "They do not need to go away. You give them something to eat."

The disciples were stunned. They knew they did not have enough money to feed all those people. When they searched through the crowd, they could find only five loaves of bread and two fish.

Jesus told them to bring Him the bread and the fish. Then He told the people to sit down on the grass. He took the food, and looking up to heaven, gave thanks for it. He began breaking the five loaves into pieces and handing them to the disciples. He told the twelve men to pass the bread out among the people. He did the same for the two fish. The crowd and the disciples kept expecting the food to run out, but Jesus continued breaking off pieces. At last the people had eaten all they could hold and were satisfied. Jesus directed the disciples to pick up the food that was left over. The broken pieces filled twelve baskets! Jesus had fed 5,000 people with just five loaves of bread and two small fish.

Have the children memorize this Bible verse and say it before eating their "Simple Lunch" (described below):

They all ate and were satisfied. (Mark 6:42)

A Simple Lunch

This activity is fun for the children to do to help them pretend to be part of the 5,000 people Jesus fed.

Materials: pita bread, fish-shaped crackers or cooked fish cakes, drinks, napkins, cups

If the weather permits, go outside for lunch. If not, have the children sit on the floor. Give each child a portion of pita bread and fish or crackers on napkins. Serve a cold fruit drink. Be sure to thank God for the meal and for Jesus and His great love. Ask children to pretend they were in the crowd of 5,000. Ask how they would have felt if they had been part of the miracle of feeding all those people with just five loaves and two fish.

One Little Boy

This fingerplay will help the children retell the story of Jesus feeding the 5,000.

This is the one little boy who shared his supper.	*(Hold up one finger.)*
These are the two little fish in his basket.	*(Hold up two fingers of other hand.)*
There are the five little loaves of bread.	*(Hold up five fingers of first hand.)*
And these are the thousands and thousands and thousands and thousands of people . . .	*(Open and shut all fingers of both hands for each "thousands." Do it faster and faster.)*
. . . who shared five loaves	*(Hold up five fingers.)*
and two fish	*(Hold up two fingers.)*
with one little boy.	*(Hold up one finger.)*

Five Loaves and Two Fish

Sing to the tune of "John Brown's Body."

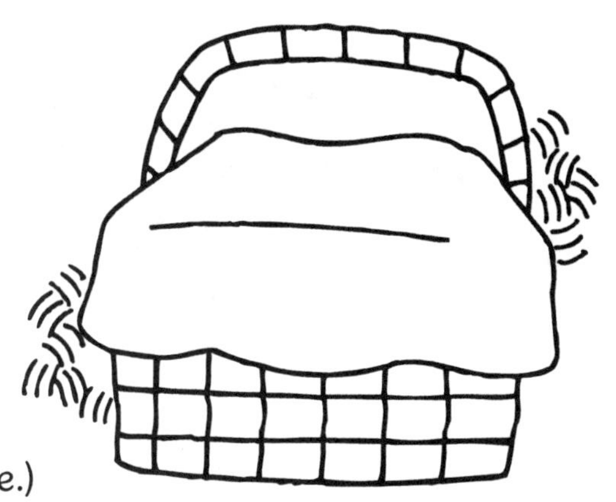

Five thousand people followed Jesus 'round the sea.
Five thousand people followed Jesus 'round the sea.
Five thousand people followed Jesus 'round the sea.
'Twas the Sea of Galilee.

One small boy had brought a basket with some lunch.
(Repeat twice.)
But how could he feed this bunch?

Five small loaves of bread and two tiny fish. (Repeat twice.)
But to share them was His wish.

"Thank You, God," said Jesus as the people shared the food. (Repeat twice.)
And they all ate and said it was good.

A Basket Full of Food

Materials:

copies of the patterns below
small paper lunch bag
crayons
scissors

Directions:

1. Give the children copies of the patterns.
2. Have the children color and cut them out.
3. Next, the children can place the two fish and five loaves in a lunch bag.
4. Discuss with the children how they think so little could feed so many.

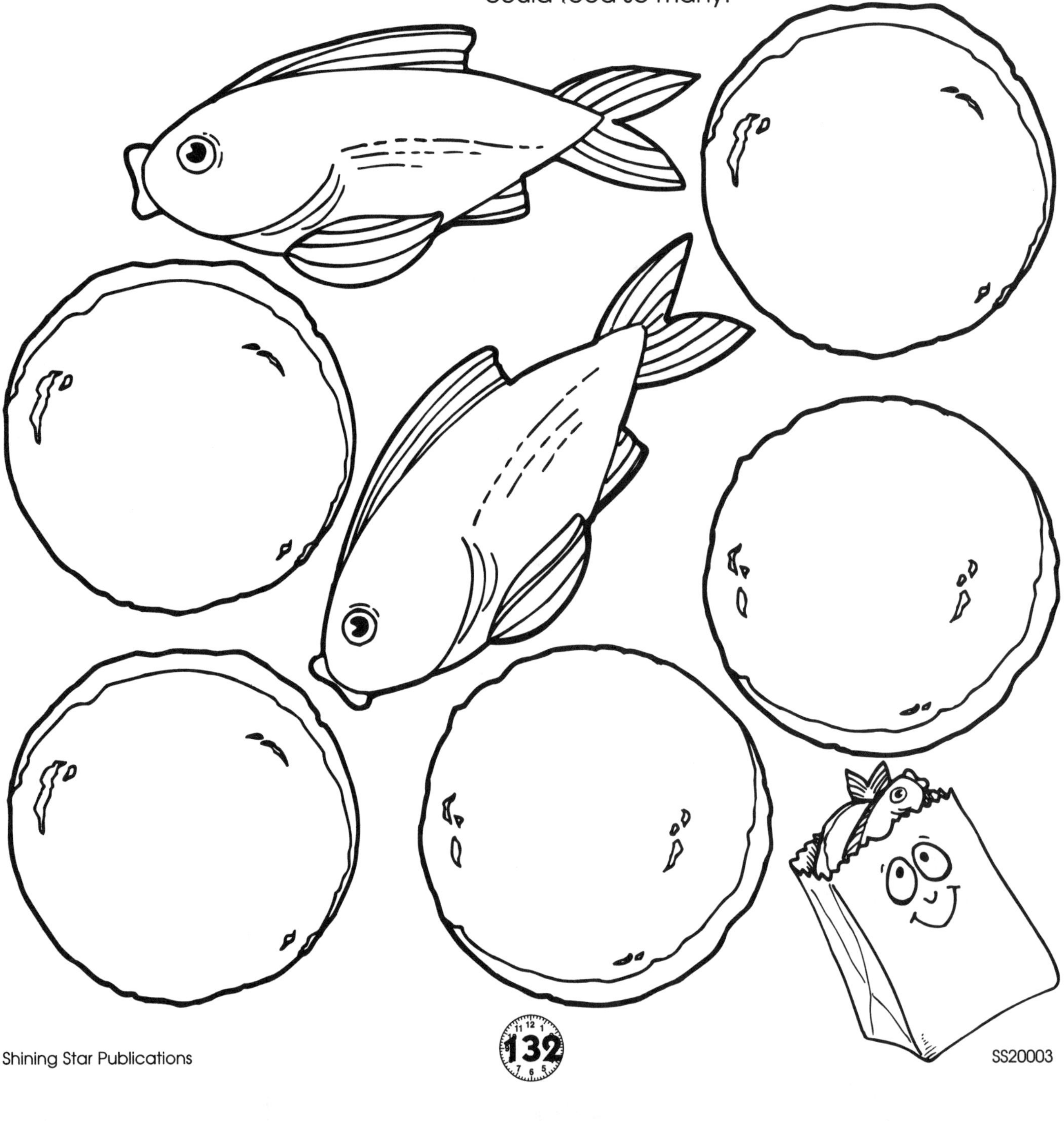

"Let Them Come to Me"

Mark 10:13–16

It was a beautiful, sunny day, not too hot, even for Israel. Jesus was teaching a group of people about His Holy Father and Himself. Some parents were trying to get through the crowd to Him because they wanted Him to bless their children. The children were probably noisy, as they sometimes are.

"Take those children away," said the disciples, "Jesus is busy!" They didn't want their Master bothered when He was doing important work.

The Lord looked at the children Himself and said, *"Let the little children come to me, and do not hinder them, for the kingdom of God belongs to such as these. I tell you the truth, anyone who will not receive the kingdom of God like a little child will never enter it."* (Mark 10:14–15)

The parents were happy as the children smiled and went to Jesus. Lovingly, He took them in His arms, put His hands on them, and blessed each one.

Jesus Loves Me!

This 3-D picture frame is fun for the children to make to remind them of Jesus' love for them.

Materials:
copies of the patterns below, crayons, scissors, glue, photo of each child (optional)

Directions:
Give the children copies of the patterns. Have them color the heart and flowers and cut them out. Tell the children to glue the cutout flowers on top of the flowers on the heart. They should apply glue only under the flower centers, allowing the petals to stand out for a 3-D effect. Have the children draw their picture or glue a small photo of themselves in the circle.

Jesus LOVES

Jesus Heals a Blind Man

Luke 18:35–43

Jesus often liked to teach outdoors. He didn't always teach inside a house or synagogue. One day, He was walking toward Jericho with a lot of other people and talking with them. As they walked, they came near a blind man sitting beside the road and begging. He had no home to go to, and he couldn't see to work. All he could do was sit there and hope somebody would give him money or food.

There was such a crowd of people around Jesus that the blind man couldn't help hearing them talk, but he could not see who it was. "What is going on?" he called out.

Somebody told him, "Jesus of Nazareth is going by."

The blind man had heard of Jesus. He knew that sometimes Jesus healed people. He thought, "This is my chance!" He shouted, "Jesus, have mercy on me."

The people around Jesus thought the blind man wasn't very polite to yell at Him like that. They thought he shouldn't bother Jesus. They told the blind man to keep still.

He didn't pay any attention to them. He jumped up and shouted again, even louder, "Jesus, Son of David, have mercy on me!" He couldn't see, so he couldn't tell which man was Jesus. If the blind man could have seen, he would have run to Jesus, knelt down, and asked more humbly for help. Instead, he just stood there and shouted.

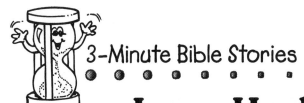

Jesus Heals . . . continued

This time, Jesus heard him. He didn't know what the blind man wanted, but He was always ready to help people. He stopped right there in the road and said to one of His friends, "Bring the man who is shouting to Me." The friend went over to the side of the road where the blind man was standing. He took the man's arm and led him to Jesus.

Jesus said to him, "Why are you asking for mercy? What do you want Me to do for you?"

The blind man replied, "Lord, I want to see! I ask You to have mercy on me and heal my eyes so I can see."

Jesus said to him, "You shall see. Because you have faith that I can help you, you are healed."

Suddenly, the man's eyes were healed, and he could see! He thanked God and praised Him as he followed Jesus. The man didn't have to sit by the side of the road and beg any more. Jesus had healed his blindness. Now he could see to work and to walk freely with people and to enjoy the beautiful world around him.

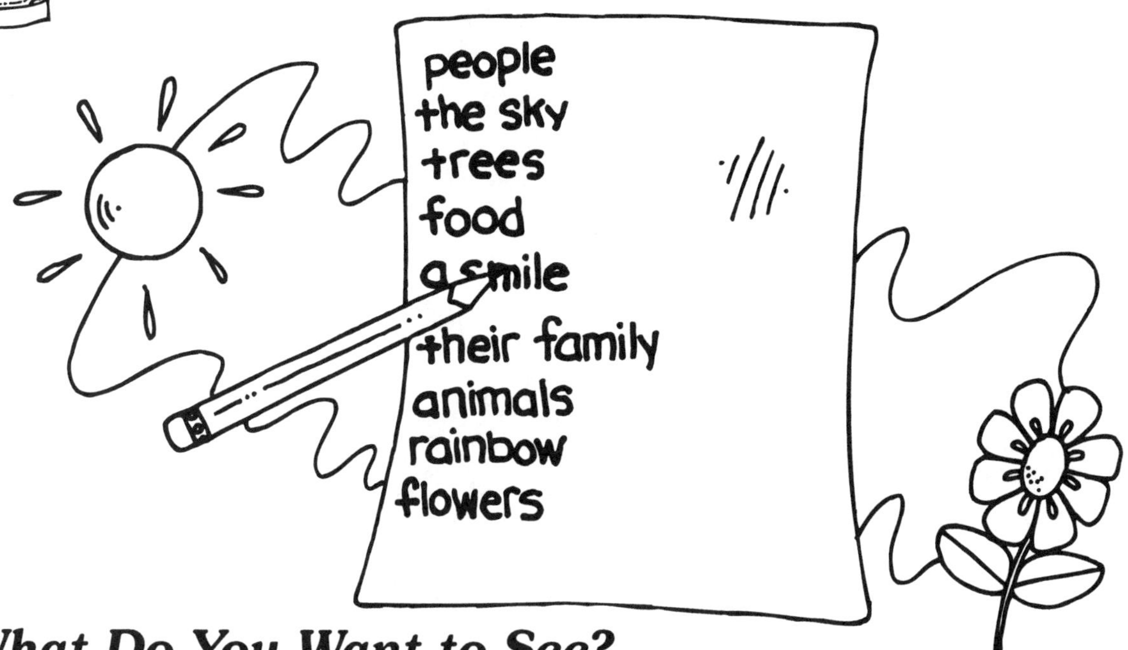

people
the sky
trees
food
a smile
their family
animals
rainbow
flowers

What Do You Want to See?

Ask the children to shut their eyes, keep their hands over them for a minute, and think about what the blind man would be most glad to see when he was healed. After opening their eyes, they can make a class list. A large class may be divided into groups who may compare their lists.

Have Mercy

Let the children improvise a skit dramatizing this story. Have one child volunteer to sit on the floor, blindfolded. Have him or her keep asking for mercy or help while the other children try to keep him or her still. Another child may represent Jesus, asking what the blindfolded one wants. When the blindfolded one answers, the child representing Jesus takes off the other's blindfold and announces his or her healing. This may be done several times with different volunteers so that more than one will have the experience of regaining his or her sight.

Seeing

Ask the children to pretend they have been blind and have just regained their sight. Sing the song below to the tune of "Three Blind Mice." It may be sung in unison or as a round.

Oh, my Lord, I can see
All the things You made for me.
I see the sun and the birds that fly.
I see the trees with their branches high.
I see the moon in the starry sky.
And I thank You.
I thank You.

A Kind Man

Luke 10:25–37

An expert in the law was questioning Jesus. When Jesus said we should love our neighbors, the lawyer asked, "Who is my neighbor?" Jesus answered by telling this story:

A man was going to Jericho when he was attacked by robbers. They beat him and took his clothes, leaving him half dead.

A priest came by on the road. He saw the man, but he did not want to get involved, so he passed by on the other side of the road. Next, a Levite rode by and saw the injured man, but he also passed by on the other side.

A Samaritan was also traveling on the road. Samaritans were not liked by Jews. When the Samaritan saw the man, he went straight to him! When he saw how badly hurt the man was, the Samaritan took pity on him. He put oil and wine on the man's wounds and bandaged them. He put the injured man on his donkey and took him to an inn. He cared for him through the night, and the next day, he gave the innkeeper two silver coins and told him to look after the man. The Samaritan said if the innkeeper needed more, he would pay it when he returned.

Jesus asked the expert in the law which of the three men was a neighbor to the man who fell into the hands of robbers. The expert replied that it was the one who showed mercy.

Jesus told him, "Go and do likewise." (Luke 10:37)

Good Neighbors

Discuss with the children people who have been "Good Samaritans" to them. The children may be eager to give examples, but if they are slow to respond, prime them with some questions, such as these: *Who is a good neighbor when you cross the street? Was somebody a good neighbor when you went to the dentist's office? Can a nurse be a good neighbor? A policeman? Does a good neighbor have to live right next to you?*

Samaritan

Form a circle with all the children except one. Blindfold that one and put him or her in the center of the circle. As he or she calls out "Jericho," the whole group circles to the right. After a few seconds, he or she calls out "Robber!" The circle stops at once, and the center child points and calls, "Neighbor!"

Whoever the center child is pointing at must tell how someone has been a neighbor to him or her. If he or she can't think of anybody, then this child becomes the blindfolded one, and the game goes on. If he or she does tell of someone's help, he or she is given a construction paper crown with a big S on it. The game continues until each child has a "Samaritan" crown or time runs out.

Help!

Have children sing this song to the tune of "Row, Row, Row Your Boat" in unison or as a round. If you want to use motions, have everybody join hands in a circle around one child lying on the floor. At the last line of the song, they all kneel and reach out their hands to the "injured" one.

Help! Help! Help the man
Lying in the dust.
To be a good Samaritan,
Help him now we must.

Tender Loving Care

There are many people today who need our help. Ask the children if they can think of some. How about the people that live in nursing homes. Can the children think of how we might be able to help them?

Tell the children that one way to show love for others is to make cookies for them. Then let the children help you make the cookies.

TLC Cookies

(The dough can be made ahead of time.)

Mix together:

¾ cup shortening (part butter)

1 cup sugar

2 eggs

1 teaspoon vanilla

Blend in:

1 ½ cups flour

1 teaspoon baking powder

1 teaspoon salt

Cover the dough; chill at least one hour.

Roll the dough ⅛" thick on a lightly floured board. Cut out with a heart-shaped cookie cutter.

Mix with fork in a small bowl the following: 2 egg yolks, ½ teaspoon water. Divide the mixture into small cups. Add a few drops of food coloring to each cup to make several different colors. Using a different paintbrush for each color, paint designs or messages on your cookies with tender loving care.

Bake at 350° for 6–8 minutes or until lightly brown; then cool.

Put the beautiful cookies in a cloth-lined basket and take them to a local nursing home. Share yourself and your cookies with your "neighbors."

A Special Card

The children will enjoy making get-well cards to give to those who are sick to cheer them up.

Materials:
copies of the pattern below, crayons, scissors, 6 ½" x 3 ½" envelopes, postage stamps

Directions:

1. Have the children color and decorate the get-well cards.
2. Next, they cut them out on the bold lines and then fold on the broken lines.
3. Tell the children to print their names and to whom they want to send their cards to on the lines.
4. The children can use the envelopes to mail their cards.

The King

Mark 11:1–11

The city of Jerusalem was full of excitement. It was time to celebrate the Feast of the Passover. People had come from miles around.

News spread that the King of the Jews was coming. Crowds began to close in—pushing, shoving, stretching their necks to see. The noise increased with the excitement, and soldiers attempted to calm the crowd. But the people only became more restless.

"He's coming!" shouted someone. "I see Him! The King! The King of the Jews!" The people began to wave palm branches as they called out, "Hosanna! Hosanna! Blessed is the King of Israel!"

A man riding on a donkey with a robe thrown over it came into view. But this man didn't look like a king. He didn't wear beautiful jewels. There was no crown on His head.

Someone called out, "Who is He?"

A voice from the excited crowd answered, "It is Jesus!"

As Jesus rode nearer, some of the people placed their palm leaves in the road. Others took off their robes and laid them in the pathway. The disciples walked proudly alongside Jesus. The crowd followed behind, singing praises. "Praise God! Hosanna!" they sang.

Not all the people were filled with joy and thanksgiving. Some of them hated Jesus. They wanted Him arrested. The cheering noise of the people angered them.

"Make these crowds be still," the Pharisees commanded Jesus. "Tell them to be quiet."

"If they keep quiet," Jesus answered, "I tell you, the very stones of Jerusalem will shout."

This made the people sing louder and shout even more praises: "Hosanna! Hosanna! Blessed is the King."

A Palm Sunday Song

Explain to the children that we celebrate the day Jesus rode into Jerusalem on a donkey on Palm Sunday. Then let the children make fans or palm leaves by folding green construction paper.

Next, teach the children the words below to the familiar tune, "Here We Go 'Round the Mulberry Bush."

Before singing, have the children form two lines, with children facing one another as if standing and waiting for a parade. Have them hold up their palm leaves or fans. As they sing the first stanza, the children should stretch their necks as if looking for Jesus to come down the road.

As they sing the second stanza of the song, they should wave the leaves up and down, and then lay them on the ground.

As they sing the third stanza, the children should cup their hands around their mouths and lift their chins upward.

Have them get down on their knees and make praying hands as they sing the last stanza.

This is the way we watch for Him, watch for Him, watch for Him.
This is the way we watch for Him on Palm Sunday morning.

This is the way we welcome Him, welcome Him, welcome Him.
This is the way we welcome Him on Palm Sunday morning.

This is the way we sing our praise, sing our praise, sing our praise.
This is the way we sing our praise on Palm Sunday morning.

This is the way we pray to Him, pray to Him, pray to Him.
This is the way we pray to Him on Palm Sunday morning.

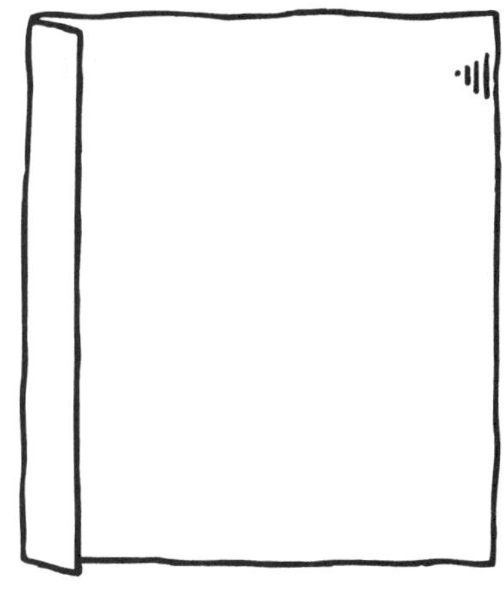

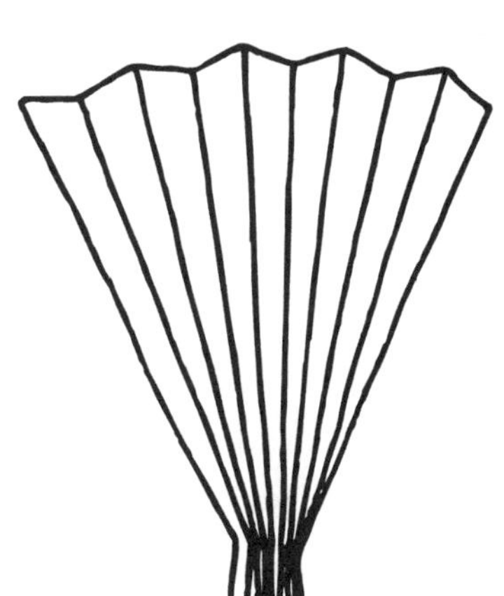

Window Ornaments

Help the children celebrate Palm Sunday by making these window ornaments.

Materials:

copies of the palm leaf pattern below
waxed paper
construction paper
tissue paper
iron, on low setting
crayon or marker
glue
pencil
scissors

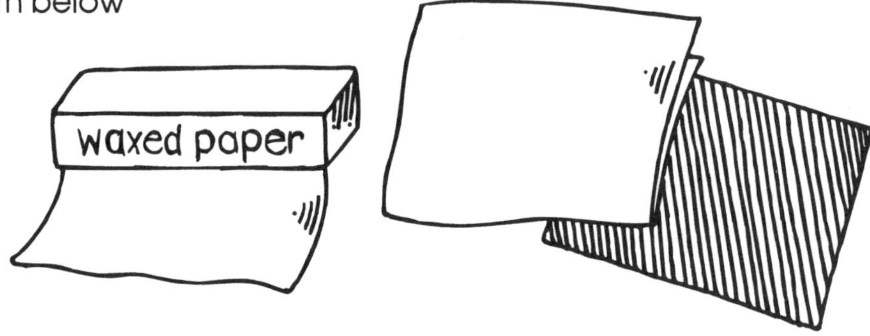

Directions:

Tear two pieces of waxed paper, about 8" long, for each child. Help the children trace around their palm leaves on green tissue paper and cut them out. They can use brown tissue paper for the stems. Tell the children to glue their palm leaves and stems on the center of one piece of waxed paper. Next, they lay their other piece of waxed paper over their leaves. Press the papers together using a warm iron. Next, cut a 7" x 7" square out of the center of a piece of construction paper for each child, discarding the squares. Then show the children how to place another sheet of construction paper under their cut ones for the frames. The children can glue their waxed paper designs between the two pieces of the frame. Help them trim away any extra waxed paper. Help the children use a crayon or marker to write "Hosanna" on their frames.

The Market in the Temple

Matthew 21:12–17

Jesus had come to the temple in Jerusalem to teach people more about God's Law. As He walked into the courtyard, He heard arguing and yelling. Doves were squawking and sheep were bleating. The temple didn't look like the house of the Lord at all. It looked like a marketplace.

Jesus stared in anger as He saw the moneychangers doing business and the bankers sitting behind tables, trading money so people could buy sacrifices. There was bustling activity everywhere, and noise, noise, noise!

All of a sudden, a heavy table came crashing over. Cage doors flew open, and doves came flapping out. Coins rolled every which way. The moneylender screamed out, "What are you doing?"

It was Jesus. He threw over a table—crash! Then another table! More animals were freed, and more money scattered. Jesus continued shoving tables and slinging money. Sheep were bleating, cows were lowing, birds were flying. Everywhere there was confusion, and Jesus was causing it.

Jesus' voice was loud and angry: "Listen, don't the Scriptures tell us what God has said? 'My house shall be a house of prayer for all people.' You've turned it into a den of robbers. I am making it clean! Take all these things out!"

The Pharisees and scribes were furious with Jesus. They were determined to get rid of Him. "We must kill this man," they said, and they began to make their plans.

Crowds gathered around Jesus. He sat and waited for them to grow quiet. A blind man was led through the crowd. Jesus' face became gentle again. He lightly touched the man's eyes, and the man could see. The people cheered. Other sick people pushed and shoved their way toward Jesus so they, too, might be made well.

There were children standing nearby, and they began shouting, "Hosanna to the Son of David!"

A Special Place

Jesus was angry because many people did not respect the house of God. They did not use the temple for worship as they were supposed to. Jesus was also angry at the Pharisees because they did not want children to be there, singing praises to the Lord. The Lord wants all His people to praise Him and worship Him.

Set aside a special place in your classroom where children may worship the Lord. Let them help you plan how to make it special. What things will you need? (Ideas: a small table, a Bible, a piece of felt to drape across the table, a rug to lay in front of the table to kneel on) Assemble these pieces and help the children make some of the items below for your worship area.

Candle and Candleholder:
Form a piece of clay into a ball. Press a hole in the ball big enough to hold a candle. Put the candle in the hole and press clay around it so it stands by itself. Make a small wreath with pine branches or flowers to put around the candleholder.

Elegant Bookmark:
Knot together, at the top, four 12" pieces of different colored hair ribbon. Use each ribbon to mark a special page in the Bible.

Cross:
Find sticks or twigs outside. Tie them together with string for a rustic-looking cross.

Centerpiece:
Go on a nature hunt and find wildflowers, bark, leaves, etc. Arrange them in a vase.

Banner:
Design a banner on a piece of paper. Transfer it to a large piece of felt. Glue a wooden dowel at the top of the banner as shown. Add yarn to hang it up.

Temple Game

Below is a fun game the children can play to learn how important the temple was to Jesus.

The children flip a coin and move ahead one space for heads and two spaces for tails. Have them read each Bible verse on which they land. The children can play alone or with a friend.

Start

"Yes," replied Jesus, "have you never read, 'From the lips of children and infants you have ordained praise'?" (Matthew 21:16b)

Go back one space.

But when the chief priests and the teachers of law saw the wonderful things he did and the children shouting in the temple area, "Hosanna to the Son of David," they were indignant. (Matthew 21:15)

Go ahead one space.

Go ahead one space.

"Do you hear what these children are saying?" they asked him. (Matthew 21:16a)

Skip a turn!

And he left them and went out of the city to Bethany, where he spent the night. (Matthew 21:17)

"It is written," he said to them, "'My house will be called a house of prayer,' but you are making it a 'den of robbers.'" (Matthew 21:13)

The blind and the lame came to him at the temple, and he healed them. (Matthew 21:14)

Go back one space.

Take an extra turn!

He overturned the tables of the money changers and the benches of those selling doves. (Matthew 21:12b)

Go back one space.

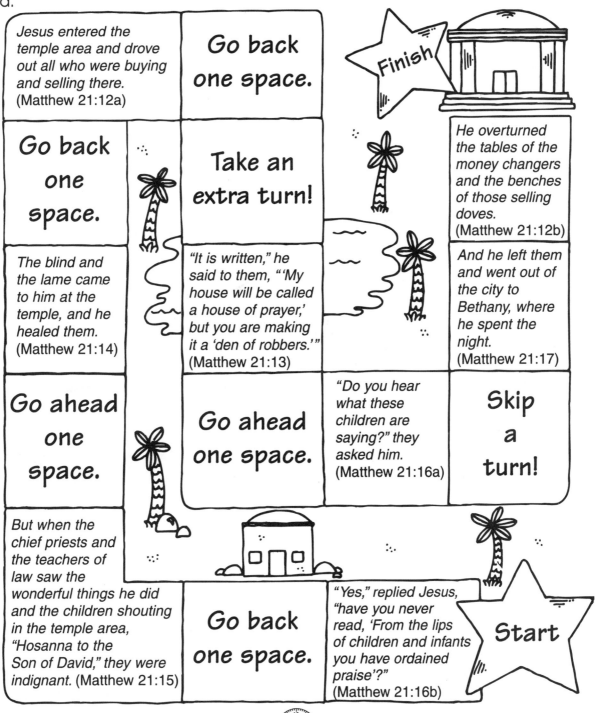

Jesus entered the temple area and drove out all who were buying and selling there. (Matthew 21:12a)

Finish

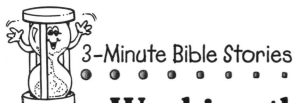

Washing the Disciples' Feet

John 13:3–17

In the days when Jesus lived in Palestine, most people walked barefoot or wore sandals. It was a warm country, so they didn't need socks and shoes. The trouble was that their feet got very hot and dusty. They needed to wash their feet when they went into anybody's house. Homeowners, to be polite, would give each guest a basin of water for washing his or her feet. If the person wanted to show special honor to someone, he or she would wash the guest's feet himself.

One evening, Jesus was having supper with His disciples. Suddenly He thought of a way to teach them. He got up from the table and took off His outer robe. He tied a towel around His waist and brought a basin of water.

Jesus washed the feet of several disciples and dried them with a towel. Peter was shocked at the idea of Jesus doing such a thing for him. He thought it should be the other way around, that he should serve Jesus.

Peter said, "Lord, are You really going to wash my feet?"

Jesus answered, "You don't realize now why I'm doing this. Later, you will understand."

"Oh no," said Peter. "You shall never wash my feet!"

"Then you cannot be one of My followers," answered Jesus.

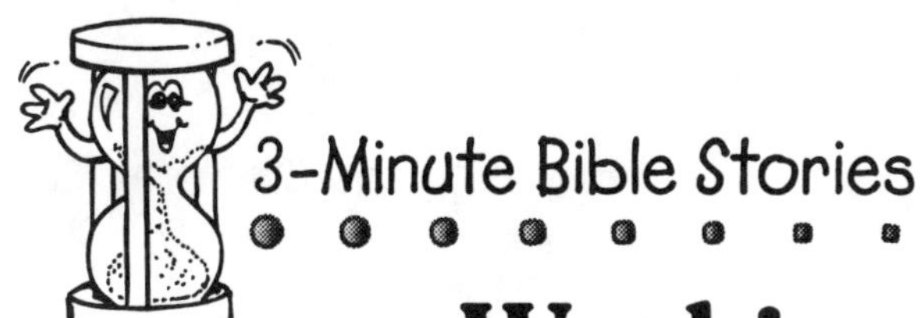

Washing . . . continued

That hurt Peter's feelings. He had wanted to be one of Jesus' followers from the day Jesus had first called him from his fishing. "If that is the way," he said, "wash my head and my hands as well."

Jesus said, "No, that is not needed." He didn't want them to think a bath was what He was talking about. He washed Peter's feet and those of the rest of the disciples. They were not sure why He was doing it, but they wanted to do whatever Jesus said they should.

When Jesus had finished, He took the towel off His waist, put on His robe again, and sat down with them. Then He explained, "I have set you an example. You should follow it. If I am your Lord and Teacher, as you call Me, then you should do as I have done for you."

Of course, He didn't mean that they should wash everybody's feet. He meant that if He was willing to do little ordinary things to help other people, His followers should be, too. He finished His teaching by saying, "Now that you know these things, you will be blessed if you do them."

Like the disciples, we need to learn what Jesus wants us to do, and we need to do things for other people as He did.

The prayer and song below will remind the children of the importance of the disciples and how Jesus once washed their feet.

My Feet

Help children read or recite this prayer; then repeat it with the motions.

Sometimes I march, *(March in place.)*
Or I tiptoe; *(Tiptoe in place.)*
Sometimes I run *(Run in place.)*
Wherever I go.

Please lead my feet
Where they should go
As You did the disciples'
So long ago.
(Stand with hands folded as if in prayer, but look down at feet as the group moves into a prayer circle.)

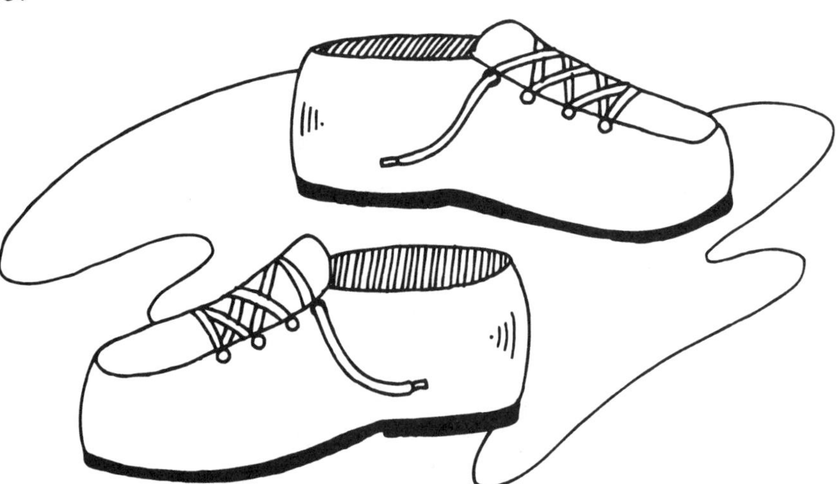

Peter Speaks

Using the motions, sing this song to the tune of "The Farmer in the Dell."

Jesus washed my feet.
Jesus washed my feet.
(Have children stand in a row and point to their feet during the first two lines.)
I was His disciple *(Put hand on heart in gesture of allegiance.)*
When Jesus washed my feet. *(Point to feet again.)*

He showed, "To serve is sweet."
He showed, "To serve is sweet."
(Hold out arms during first two lines.)
I am His disciple, *(Put hand on heart again.)*
For Jesus washed my feet. *(Keep hand on heart while pointing to feet again with other hand.)*

The Last Supper

Matthew 26:17–30; Mark 14:12–26

Families and friends all over Jerusalem gathered to celebrate the Passover Feast. In each house, people celebrated with roasted lamb, unleavened bread, side dishes, and bitter herbs.

While the rest of the city of Jerusalem was enjoying the celebration, Jesus sat with His 12 disciples in a quiet upper room. Jesus was at the head of the table. When the meal was about to begin, Jesus did not tell His disciples the Passover story as they had expected. Instead, Jesus began, "I tell you the truth, one of you is going to betray Me tonight."

The disciples were confused, "How could that be?" They loved Jesus. They would never betray Him. "Surely not I, Lord," each one said.

John asked, "Lord, who is it?"

Jesus answered, "It is the one to whom I will give this piece of bread when I have dipped it in the dish." Then He dipped the bread and handed it to Judas Iscariot.

"Surely not I, Teacher?" said the man who was about to betray His Lord for 30 silver coins.

"Yes," answered Jesus, "it is you. What you are about to do, go and do quickly." Judas left and went to talk to the Pharisees to tell them where they could go to capture Jesus.

While they were eating, Jesus took some bread, blessed it, and began breaking it into pieces. Then He passed the broken bread to each of His disciples. He said, "Take and eat, for this is My body which is broken for you."

Then Jesus lifted the goblet of wine. After blessing it, He passed it to each of His disciples saying, "Take and drink. This is My blood which is shed for the forgiveness of sins."

This was a very important occasion that Jesus didn't want His disciples to ever forget. "As often as you eat this bread and drink this wine," He said, "remember Me."

After Jesus and His disciples sang a hymn, they left and went to the Mount of Olives to a garden to pray.

"Reminders of God" Quilt

To help the children remember Jesus as He wants them to, make a class quilt with different colored pieces of construction paper as patches. Have the children color pictures of things that remind them of God. Have them sign their "patches" and glue them several inches apart to a big piece of butcher paper. Draw small lines around each picture to look like thread marks.

A Special Supper

Bring in some bread (pita bread or an uncut loaf) that may be torn into pieces and some grape juice. After washing their hands, have children sit around a table. Pass around the loaf of bread. Let each child tear off his or her own portion. Then hand out small paper cups of grape juice.

Remind the children that when the Jews celebrated the Last Supper, they "retold" the story of how God used Moses to lead His chosen people out of slavery in Egypt and into the Promised Land.

After eating the bread and drinking the juice, allow each child to "retell" a favorite Bible story.

The Capture of Jesus

Matthew 26:36–56; Mark 14:32–52; Luke 22:47–53; John 18:1–11

Jesus prayed in the Garden of Gethsemane. His heart was heavy on this night. He knew He would soon be suffering for the sins of the whole world. "Father, everything is possible because of You. Take this cup from Me."

Jesus knew that God had the power to instantly take Him up to heaven with Him. There would be no pain or suffering there. But Jesus knew why God had sent Him to earth. He knew He must suffer and die so that all men might be saved. Jesus ended His prayer by saying, "Do not do what I want, but what You want."

While Jesus prayed, the disciples slept nearby. Even though Jesus had asked them to keep watch, they could not stay awake even for one hour. Jesus walked over to where they were lying. "Are you still sleeping and resting?" He asked. "Enough! The hour has come. Let us go! Here comes my betrayer!"

As He was speaking, the lights of many torches came into view. Soldiers armed with swords and clubs pushed forward. Chief priests and Pharisees walked behind them.

Jesus asked them, "Who is it you want?"

"Jesus of Nazareth," they replied.

Judas, one of the disciples, was standing with the chief priests. He stepped forward and kissed Jesus on the cheek. This was the sign for the soldiers to know who they were to arrest. Judas had betrayed his teacher and master, an innocent man, for 30 silver coins.

Jesus looked into the eyes of Judas and said, "Do you betray Me with a kiss?"

With that, the soldiers stepped forward to arrest Jesus. Peter quickly took his sword and lashed out at one of the high priests, cutting off his ear.

"Put your sword back in its place." Jesus said to him . . . (Matthew 26:52) He touched the man's ear and healed him. "Don't you know that I could call on My Father and He would send thousands of angels to rescue Me?" Jesus said. He wanted His disciples to understand. "But God's Word says that it must happen this way. So let it be as He has said."

Prayer Banner

Jesus knew He had to be arrested to fulfill what His Father wanted to happen. Let the children make the banners below to remind them of God's will.

Materials:

copies of the patterns below
felt (blue, white, and black)
glue
yarn
black marker
pencil
scissors
hole punch

Directions:

1. Trim an 8" x 11" piece of blue felt in a banner shape for each child.
2. Help the children trace and cut out the figure of Jesus on a white piece of felt. (Use black felt for His shadow.)
3. Tell the children to glue the figures on the banner as shown.
4. Then they (or you) can use a marker to write Jesus' words, "Not My will, but Yours be done." on the banner.
5. Help the children punch holes at the top of the banner and tie with yarn for hanging.

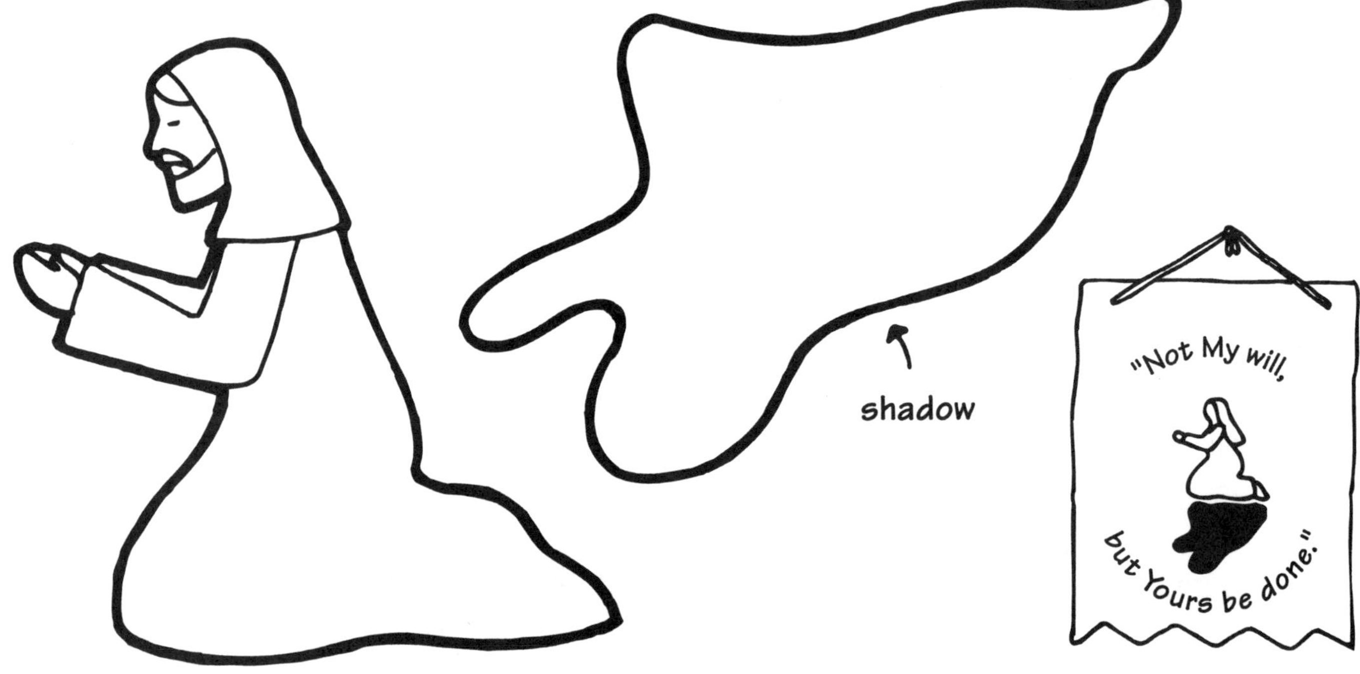
shadow
"Not My will,
but Yours be done."

Jesus Before Pilate

Mark 15:1–20; Luke 23:1–25; John 18:28–40; 19:1–16

Whips stung Jesus' skin. Blood and sweat dripped down His back. The soldiers pushed and shoved, laughing and making fun of Him.

"So, You are the King?" they sneered. "You don't look like a king. You have no robe, no crown." They spoke with hatred. The soldiers had taken Jesus' clothes. He was beaten and bruised, but Jesus stood silently before them.

The soldiers found a purple robe and laid it on Jesus' blistered back. A branch of thorns was twisted into a circle and pushed hard onto His head. Blood dripped down His face.

The soldiers continued to mock Him: "Hail, King of the Jews!" They spun Him around in circles, struck Him in the face, and spat on Him.

Then Jesus was sent to the governor, Pilate. Pilate didn't hate Jesus as the others did. He felt sorry for Him. He asked Him questions, hoping that Jesus would give the right answers so he could let Him go. "Are you the King of the Jews?"

"Yes, I am," Jesus replied.

"Don't You hear how many things they are accusing You of?"

Jesus was silent.

Pilate could find no fault with Jesus and wanted to let Him go. Each year at Passover, it was the governor's custom to let one prisoner go free. Pilate thought this would be a good chance to release Jesus. So he asked the people if they wanted him to set Jesus free.

Another man named Barabbas was also a prisoner. The elders and chief priests wanted Jesus to die. They led the crowd by shouting, "Barabbas! We want you to set Barabbas free!" The people's voices joined in and grew louder.

Pilate was confused as he spoke to the crowd. "What shall I do, then, with Jesus who is called Christ?"

They all answered, "Crucify Him!"

"But what has He done?" asked Pilate.

The crowd only shouted louder, "Crucify Him, crucify Him!"

When Pilate saw that the crowd would not change their minds, he knew what must be done. He called for a bowl of water, then washed his hands in front of the people. "I am innocent of this man's blood," he said. "It is your responsibility."

The people answered, "Let His blood be on us and on our children."

Pilate released Barabbas and handed Jesus over to be crucified.

Spring in a Bag

Easter and the events surrounding it, like Jesus' arrest and crucifixion, are celebrated each spring. Although these are not happy events, let the children try the activity below that is more joyous and that will remind them of spring.

1. Give each child a paper bag with his or her name on it. Take a spring walk to observe and collect some wonderful things God has made, such as grass, clover, wildflowers, leaves, twigs, and ladybugs.
2. While the children are collecting, have them take a deep breath, smell the different things they find, and close their eyes and touch the items.
3. Encourage the children to name all the different colors they see around them.
4. Seat children in a circle on the grass. Have them close their eyes and listen. What sounds do they hear that are God's sounds? People's sounds? Which are better?
5. Have the children lie down on their backs, look up at the sky, and watch the clouds move, noticing how they change shape.
6. Talk about the air. Does it feel cold, hot, "tickly," dry, wet? Let the children take off their shoes to feel the air with their feet.
7. Have each child crouch down and look around to see what the world is like to a little bug or animal.
8. Encourage the children to share their thoughts about the spring day and the wonderful world God has made.
9. The items that are placed in the bags may be taken back to the classroom and shared, then taken home.

Clothespin Lamb

Explain to the children that Jesus was called the Lamb of God because He died like a sacrificial lamb for our sins.

Materials:
two spring-type clothespins (per child), tongue depressors (one per child), black paint and paintbrushes, cotton balls, glue

Directions:
1. Help the children paint the bottoms of their clothespins and one end of their tongue depressors black.
2. Each child should place the tongue depressor between the two clothespins to form the body of a lamb (with the black end of the tongue depressor sticking out).
3. Tell the children to glue cotton balls to the body of the lamb. (Children should make sure to leave the black part of the tongue depressor showing for the lamb's face.)

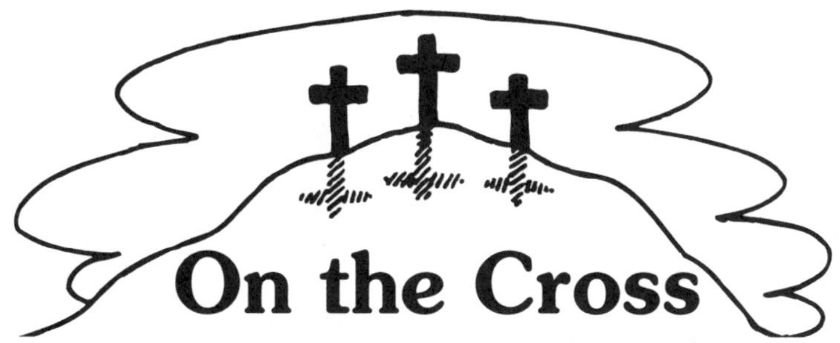

On the Cross

Matthew 27:32–55; Mark 15:21–40; Luke 23:26–49; John 19:17–30

The sun came up as usual. The sounds of a rooster crowing could be heard. Soldiers had whipped Jesus until late into the night. A tired, aching Jesus limped along the path, dragging a heavy wooden cross. He weaved back and forth until at last, He fell near a man named Simon. The soldiers forced Simon to carry Jesus' cross. Many people followed behind as they made their way to a hill called the Skull.

Two other men, both criminals, were crucified next to Jesus—one on His right, the other on His left.

As Jesus hung on the cross, the rulers said, "He saved others; let Him save Himself if He is the Son of God, the chosen one."

Jesus was not full of hatred for the people around Him. He felt pity. *Jesus said, "Father, forgive them, for they do not know what they are doing."* (Luke 23:34)

Pilate had a sign placed above Jesus' head. It read, "This is the King of the Jews."

Some people made fun of Jesus while He hung on the cross in great pain. One of the robbers hanging next to Jesus shouted cruel remarks. The other robber spoke out, "We are getting what we deserve, but this man has done nothing wrong." He slowly turned his head to Jesus and said, "Remember me when You come into Your Kingdom."

Jesus answered him, "Today you will be with Me in paradise."

Mary, Jesus' mother, stood weeping at the foot of the cross. What sadness she felt as she saw her son dying. Jesus' disciple John stood beside her.

When Jesus saw His mother and His disciple, He said, "Dear woman, this is your son." Jesus said to John, "This is your mother." From that time on, John took Mary into his home.

The hours passed as Jesus' pain continued to grow. At noon, darkness came upon the whole world for three hours. God's creation was mourning the death of His Son.

Jesus cried out in a loud voice, *"My God, my God, why have you forsaken me?"* (Mark 15:34) Then he whispered, "I am thirsty."

A soldier standing by fastened a sponge on a stick and soaked it in wine vinegar. He gave it to Jesus. After Jesus' lips had tasted the wine, He said, "It is finished. *Father, into your hands I commit my spirit."* (Luke 23:46) Then He died.

Below are some fun activities the children can do to remind themselves that Jesus died on the cross for us.

Decorative Cross

1. Two craft sticks can be glued together to form a cross.
2. Using markers, stickers, glitter, macaroni, small buttons, or other things, let the children decorate their crosses.
3. To make a hanger, a pop-top ring or a small loop of string can be glued on the back of the top of each cross.

Cookie Treats

Bake cross-shaped cutout cookies. Let the children decorate them with icing and cookie sprinkles.

Sand Art

The children can use pencils to draw pictures of three crosses on a hill. Help them squirt white glue in thin lines over their pencil marks. Then they can sprinkle plain or colored dry sand all over their papers. Let the glue dry until it feels hard when you touch it. Have the children shake the loose sand off the paper.

An Empty Tomb

Matthew 28:1–8

It was very early on the morning of the third day after Jesus was crucified. It was a beautiful morning; the sun was just coming up. However, two women walking quickly toward Jesus' tomb hardly noticed the sunshine.

They had left very early and walked all the way from the village. "There's the garden," said one. "We're getting close." They walked a little faster.

When they got to the tomb, the women had a surprise. The big stone, blocking the entrance to the tomb, was rolled away! They walked up to the tomb and saw an angel sitting on the tombstone. He was wearing a spotless, sparkling white robe. The soldiers who were supposed to be guarding the tomb had run away.

"Do not be afraid," the angel said to the women. "I know you are looking for Jesus, who was crucified. He is not here; He has risen! Come and see the place where He lay. Then go quickly and tell His disciples that He is going ahead of them into Galilee. He will see them there."

Jesus had been dead, but God had given Him new life! Filled with joy, the women rushed off to tell the disciples that Jesus was alive!

He Has Risen!

Let the children complete the resurrection picture below to remember that even though Jesus died for us, He rose from the dead. Tell them this is why we celebrate Easter.

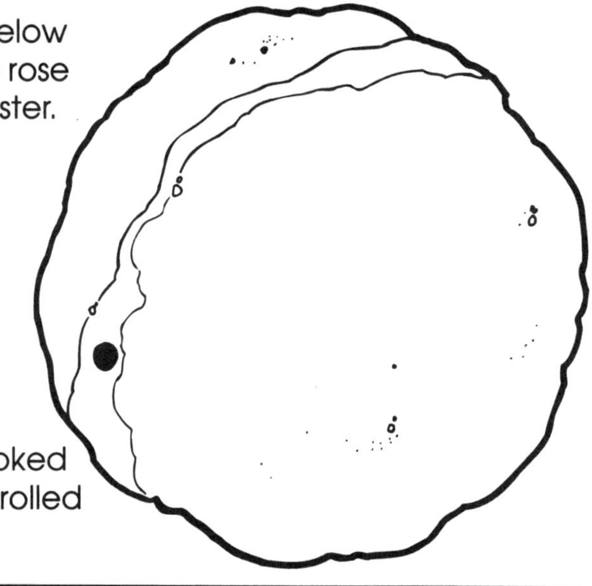

Materials:
copies of the stone pattern and picture below, crayons, scissors, brad fasteners

Directions:

1. Have the children color the "stone" and the picture below and cut them both out.
2. Help the children attach the stone to the entrance of the tomb, using a brad fastener poked through the two black dots. The stone may be rolled away from the tomb, then closed again.

Jesus
Lives!